FIRST
‹ AND ›
GOAL

JᴀKE BYRNE
with H. MICHAEL

HARVEST HOUSE PUBLISHERS
EUGENE, OREGON

Cover by Left Coast Design, Portland, Oregon

FIRST AND GOAL
Copyright © 2015 Jake Byrne
Published by Harvest House Publishers
Eugene, Oregon 97402
www.harvesthousepublishers.com

Library of Congress Cataloging-in-Publication Data
Byrne, Jake.
First and goal / Jake Byrne with H. Michael.
   pages cm
ISBN 978-0-7369-6189-9 (pbk.)
ISBN 978-0-7369-6190-5 (eBook)
1. Teenage boys—Religious life—Meditations. 2. Devotional literature. 3 Football—Miscellanea.
I. Title.
BV4541.3.B97 2015
242'.632—dc23

                                                                    2014038257

Printed in the United States of America

        15 16 17 18 19 20 21 22 23 / VP-JH / 10 9 8 7 6 5 4 3 2 1

Contents

*"Success isn't owned.
It's leased,
and rent is due every day."*

J. J. WATT

Introduction

God Arms Me with Strength

It is God who arms me with strength and keeps my way secure. He makes my feet like the feet of a deer; he causes me to stand on the heights. He trains my hands for battle; my arms can bend a bow of bronze. You make your saving help my shield, and your right hand sustains me; your help has made me great. You provide a broad path for my feet, so that my ankles do not give way. I pursued my enemies and overtook them... You armed me with strength for battle; you humbled my adversaries before me. You made my enemies turn their backs in flight, and I destroyed my foes (Psalm 18:32-40).

I received these verses from Psalm 18 in a text from my mom before one of my NFL games. The words grabbed me and put into perspective what God will do and what I need to do.

The start of a game is the calm before the storm, a time for players to prepare their minds and bodies for what is to come and embrace what we, as professionals, have trained for so long to do.

In some ways a game is like a battle. I need feet like a deer and a broad path so my ankles do not give way. I face enemies who want to destroy me, but it's God who arms me with strength for football and in life.

For all of us, life can sometimes seem like a series of battles. As an athlete with an autoimmune disease, I've faced many adversaries on the field and in life; from getting diagnosed with type 1 diabetes while chasing my goal of playing high school football to getting cut from NFL teams not once but several times.

In my freshman year in college, I was challenged with juggling academics, diabetes, and a demanding football schedule. I've embraced my plans and set big goals, but I've faced failures along the way too.

No one gets an easy pass in life. We all meet struggles while pursuing our dreams. Sometimes our knees shake when facing giants, and sometimes our feet get knocked out from under us.

Those are defining moments.

But as the psalmist reminds us, it's God who arms us and keeps our way secure. When knocked down, we must not sit and cower. God equips us with the confidence. There is peace in knowing that no matter how hard we fall, God reaches out His hand, like a teammate in a game, and pulls us back onto our feet. We make plans, but sometimes He rewrites those plans and shows us new ways to achieve our goals.

I'm surprised anyone would offer me a contract to write a book. I'm also surprised, as many of my friends will be, that my book is a devotional filled with Scripture. There's so much about religion I still don't know, but the simple fact is that deep down my faith is real, and I trust in God above all things.

First and Goal: What Football Taught Me About Never Giving Up is an A-to-Z football terminology devotional. I hope you will be encouraged through short anecdotes from my childhood, my struggles as a type 1 diabetic, and my journey in the NFL. Even if you know nothing about football, you may enjoy picking up basic terminology about the game. I pray you find comfort and strength in the Scriptures and realize that you are never alone in whatever goals you are striving to achieve.

Life is short. Now is the time to accomplish that goal you hold in your heart. With God, nothing is impossible.

Audible

When the quarterback changes the play at the line
of scrimmage, based on the defensive formation, he
calls an audible, which is a better-suited play.

Beginning my freshman year in high school, through hard work, dedication, and by the grace of God I'd earned a starting spot as an offensive tackle on our football team. Standing at 6 feet 5 and weighing in as a 240-pound 14-year-old, I was one of the team's biggest players. With early interest from college scouts, I ran full steam ahead, thinking I had life all figured out.

By the time the season had ended, I'd dropped 40 pounds and suffered from constant fatigue. The drastic weight loss confused me, my parents, and the coaches. I ate like a ravenous wolf and worked out constantly, hoping to gain weight. Instead, I shed pounds like a German shepherd sheds fur.

An unseen offense had launched a full-scale attack against my body. First, relentless hunger and weight loss. Then, the thirst. I guzzled gallons of Gatorade and water. My constant bathroom breaks annoyed my teachers and had me worried.

At the doctor's office I expected a prescription for a bladder infection. Instead, I got rocked by the hardest hit I'd ever taken: a diagnosis of type 1 diabetes.

> "I know the plans I have for you," declares the LORD, "plans
> to prosper you and not to harm you, plans to give you hope
> and a future" (Jeremiah 29:11).

Diabetes meant a major lifestyle change. My endocrinologist assured me I could still play football—but only if I did everything by the book. I had to call my own audible. This disease forced me onto my own personal line of scrimmage, where I had to come up with a new game plan and change my mind-set. Controlling my blood sugar meant huge dietary adjustments. I had to act as my own pancreas, injecting proper amounts of insulin each time I consumed carbs in order to maintain healthy sugar levels.

Support from family, friends, and coaches carried me through difficult moments, along with a peaceful reassurance that God cared about my plans, hopes, and dreams. Have you been there? Believed you had your game plan all figured out, only to take a hit from an unexpected challenge? Have faith and listen to the audible God is calling. Trust that He has plans for you—good plans for a future and greater plans than you can ever imagine.

Automatic First Down

Certain penalties grant the team an automatic
first down no matter the down or distance of the
play. After the penalty, yardage is determined
and players start with a new set of downs.

Just before suiting up for a high school home game, I remembered my mom's advice. She always reminded me to pray for protection as I put on my pads, laced up my shoes, and pulled on my helmet. I lowered my head in prayer.

Later on the field, I was targeted to receive the ball on a pass route. Expecting to be the hero, I reached for the ball, but a linebacker with a different plan took my legs out from under me. My moment of glory disappeared in an instant. The hit forced my body into a complete flip. Another hit came from the strong safety running at full speed.

> *Put on the full armor of God, so that when the day of evil comes, you may be able to stand your ground, and after you have done everything, to stand. Stand firm then, with the belt of truth buckled around your waist, with the breastplate of righteousness in place, and with your feet fitted with the readiness that comes from the gospel of peace. In addition to all this, take up the shield of faith, with which you can extinguish all the flaming arrows of the evil one. Take the helmet of salvation and the sword of the Spirit, which is the word of God (Ephesians 6:13-17).*

Lying on the ground and realizing with relief that I was still in one piece, I thanked God for His protection. I struggled to my feet and the crowd cheered. The refs signaled and then penalized the defense. We received an automatic first down, and I went on to score a touchdown on the next drive.

If not for God's protection and my equipment, I might have ended up with serious injuries that could have taken me out of the game I love.

In his letter to the Ephesians, the apostle Paul tells us to put on the full armor of God to avoid the schemes of the devil, who desires to take us out of the game of life.

Truth and the breastplate of righteousness—being right with God—strengthen us in all our endeavors. We need the shoes of preparation on any of life's fields, along with the shield of faith—like football pads—to protect against the enemy's attacks. The helmet of salvation, like a football helmet, also keeps us safe.

Praying each day and putting on the full armor of God will help us gain an automatic first down—a deeper connection in God's zone—and a sure win on any playing field.

Balanced Line

A balanced line consists of five linemen. The center
is positioned in the middle with a guard and tackle
on either side. A tight end can be added to either
side, making that side of the line the strong side.

I was two years old when I saved my sister's life. (I'm not sure if I actually remember the incident or just the story that was told to me.) Baby Betsy, seated in her rolling activity walker, was headed straight for the open basement door. I rushed toward her, grabbed the back of the walker, and screamed for my mom. I'd reached her just as the walker, balanced on the edge of the top step, threatened to crash down to a cement floor.

> *Greater love has no one than this: to lay down one's life for one's friends (John 15:13).*

A balanced line is just as important in life as it is in football. You need to keep a balanced life, but sometimes you need added strength—someone who cares—much like adding a tight end to make your strong side.

Grabbing hold of Betsy's walker, and using my toddler strength to hold her in balance, kept her from crashing down the stairs. But since then, my sister has often been the strong side for me, keeping me in balance. As kids, whenever the story was told about my saving her, she would claim she saved me by teaching me how to pretend.

Most of our growing-up years were spent in the boonies, and being only 18 months apart, we were best friends. Betsy and I would play for hours with her Barbies and my G.I. Joe. (I refused to play with Ken, but Joe may have served Barbie tea beside her pink pool a time or two.)

"Pretend this, Jake," she would say. Always the pragmatic, serious big brother, I needed Betsy's sassy-but-easygoing personality to balance me. As teenagers and beyond, her feminine perspective helped me in my relationships, and my masculine viewpoint helped her (when she would listen to me).

You probably won't be called to actually lay down your life for someone, but pulling each other out of a bad spot by being the strong end, or just stepping up to serve another, makes for a balanced life. And being balanced keeps us steady on the path toward our goals.

Ball Carrier

Any player who has possession of the ball.
While usually a running back, wide receiver, or
quarterback, this term can include any player who
happens to end up with the football in his hands.

"Tere is no cure." The doctor set down his pen and folded his hands. It took a moment for his words to register, for me to understand that no pill or diet could fix me. My throat tightened. I rested my head in my hands. Fourteen years old and stuck with type 1 diabetes. Life as I knew it was over.

But that moment of hopelessness didn't last long. Being a stubborn teenager worked in my favor. I said a prayer, asking God for help. By the time I got into the car, I had decided I was not going to let diabetes rule me. I couldn't get rid of the disease, but with God's help I could control it and still be a ball carrier—in football and with this disease.

Counting carbs, constantly checking my blood sugar, and injecting insulin proved to be a hard adjustment but a necessary part of my new normal. I chose to take responsibility for my health and not look back. Emotions that didn't gain me positive yards became obstacles to my goal.

Jesus replied, "No one who puts a hand to the plow and looks back is fit for service in the kingdom of God" (Luke 9:62).

Plowing through life, you're bound to run into obstructions. Some of life's trials result from mistakes and missteps, and some from poor choices. I know about that too, because I've made my share of blunders and had to face the consequences.

Other times, the unexpected lands in your hands like a wayward ball and the "trouble" coming at you is like a 250-pound linebacker blitzing straight off the edge.

As the ball carrier of whatever passes life throws your way—good or bad, no matter the origin—don't give up. Turn to God, keep your hand to the plow, and work hard. Jesus promises to carry us through anything and even turn trouble into good. His love will always lift us back onto our feet, but we have to do our part—carry the ball, look forward, and plow through life toward the goal line.

Blindsided

A player is blindsided when he takes an unexpected
hit that surprises him.

On the Houston Texans' roster, after playing for nine weeks and
getting reps in each game, I breathed easier, feeling a sense of job
security in the NFL. Then I got the flu. I missed one midweek practice to go to the hospital. That cost me my spot on the roster. A health-
ier tight end on the practice squad was activated, and I was released
to clear waivers. (Clear waivers means other teams have the option to
sign a cut player to their 53-man roster. If no one takes the player, other
teams can offer a spot on their practice squad.)

So, while the rest of my teammates flew to Indianapolis to play
the Colts, I sat in my apartment, blindsided and uncertain about my
future in the NFL.

> *When I am afraid, I put my trust in you. In God, whose
> word I praise—in God I trust and am not afraid. What
> can mere mortals do to me? (Psalm 56:3-4).*

Just as I could not control getting the flu, I couldn't do anything to
change my current situation after being cut from the regular season roster. I chose to trust God and give the situation to Him. Then I thanked
God, sank onto my couch, and relaxed with the latest Madden Football video game, playing the Colts versus Texans. Able to choose myself
as the player, I threw the ball to my virtual self every play, catching 20
balls for nearly 400 yards, and getting 6 touchdowns.

A career game!

Singlehanded, I won the game for the Texans. I leaped to my feet
and yelled, "'Merica!" out my patio door. Minutes after that the phone
rang. An offer came from the Kansas City Chiefs.

The Bible tells us to trust in God and not be afraid. Fear can paralyze us when we land in unexpected circumstances. If this happens to you, take a step back and look at the situation. Is there anything you can do to change it? If not, trust in God and then let go. Relax with a video game, go for a walk, or maybe yell out an empowering phrase. But ultimately, trust that an answer will come. It may not happen as quickly as it did for me, but God answers prayers. And with God, there's nothing to fear.

Blitz

A defensive play where a team sends more than
the usual defensive linemen after the opposing
quarterback. A blitz will usually see a linebacker
or defensive back provide extra pressure on the
quarterback in hopes of disrupting the play.

Initially, I took on a positive attitude with my diabetes diagnosis. It shattered at 4:30 one morning while cooking breakfast. Spring practice had begun, and I had to be on the field at 5:30, which meant I had to wake up at 4:00 to get my blood sugar right and then make breakfast with the precise amount of carbs to keep my system regulated throughout practice. I knew my parents would do anything to help, but that morning I wanted to go it on my own.

I burned the eggs while checking my blood sugar. It was too high, even though I'd taken insulin earlier. My knees felt weak. Blood sugar levels or overwhelming circumstances? I leaned against the counter. Tears stung the back of my eyes. I just wanted to be like everyone else and get to practice on time. Too many obstacles pounded me at once. About to be taken down, I slammed my fist on the counter. "Why me, God?"

Footfalls sounded in the hallway. I turned and saw my dad. Though I was bigger than him, I fell into his arms and cried like a baby.

"It'll be alright, Jake," he assured me. "We're in this together."

> *He withdrew about a stone's throw beyond them, knelt down and prayed. "Father, if you are willing, take this cup from me; yet not my will, but yours be done." An angel from heaven appeared to him and strengthened him (Luke 22:41-43).*

Like a quarterback about to get blitzed, it's easy to become overwhelmed when circumstances feel like more than the usual defensive players are pulverizing you. Jesus, knowing He was about to face a horrible crucifixion, grew overwhelmed in the garden. The Bible says His sweat became like drops of blood. God sent angels to minister to Him and strengthen Him.

My dad, like an angel, ministered to me that morning. After his reassuring words, I felt strengthened, confident I could face the challenges of life with diabetes.

Feeling defeated? Too many obstacles hitting you? Wish God would just take all the burdens away? Don't give up. Pray, like Jesus did. Maybe you'll still have to face the mountain before you, but God will send an angel in some form to minister to you and strengthen you.

Camp

A place of two-a-day practices, and you live,
eat, and breathe football from sunup to sundown
a month before the start of the season.

I hate camp. It's the hardest, most horrible part of football season, a time when you plan on physically, mentally, and emotionally breaking down. Days are measured in one-hour increments, with only twenty minutes of cherished free time. You lose track of days and forget there's an outside world. You sleep for a few hours and then throw down some ibuprofen just to get out of bed the next morning. You welcome any small distraction to take your mind off camp stressors.

During one college camp, a lineman limped into the locker room with a sprained ankle. "Man, I could go for mini corn dogs. If I had some mini corn dogs, I bet I'd heal up by tomorrow."

We all laughed, and for the next few days we joked about mini corn dogs having healing powers. When we were tired, we'd say, "If I had a mini corn dog, I'd have more energy." The jokes got us through the day.

At the end of the week, when we sat down to dinner, all eyes went to the trays on the table, where browned-to-perfection mini corn dogs cuddled up against a variety of dipping sauces.

"This is the best thing that's ever happened to me." A lineman wiped a tear from his eye.

"It's like Christmas," I said, all choked up.

"I love you, Coach." The quarterback's bottom lip quivered.

We dove into the pile of savory sausages, watched NFL football, and forgot our aches, pains, and camp struggles.

The Lord is my shepherd; I shall not want. He maketh me
to lie down in green pastures: he leadeth me beside the still
waters. He restoreth my soul: he leadeth me in the paths

21

of righteousness for his name's sake. Yea, though I walk through the valley of the shadow of death, I will fear no evil: for thou art with me; thy rod and thy staff they comfort me. Thou preparest a table before me in the presence of mine enemies: thou anointest my head with oil; my cup runneth over. Surely goodness and mercy shall follow me all the days of my life: and I will dwell in the house of the LORD for ever (Psalm 23:1-6 KJV).

For football players, camp is the valley of the shadow of death. At the college level, we doubt we will survive the week. At the professional level, many don't, as that's the time the number of players gets cut from the 80s down to the 53-man roster.

There may not be mini corn dogs on the table God prepares for us, but He promises to fill our cups and give us goodness and mercy.

Are you wondering if you will reach your goal…or even get through the day? Psalm 23 assures us that even in our darkest valley, the Lord is there, tending to our needs and setting before us the things He knows we need for encouragement and restoration. He is our Shepherd. Mini corn dogs are great, but they can't restore our souls. Only Jesus can do that.

Carry

A carry is when the player with possession
of the ball runs to gain yards.

My little brother leaned against me in the back of the SUV. "Aren't we there yet? I'm starved, bored, and tired."

The most popular words in his five-year-old vocabulary covered how I felt too. A day earlier, we'd left our home in Michigan and rode all the way to Northwest Arkansas to find a new house after my dad's job transfer. After a long day in the vehicle, stopping to view several homes, I looked forward to the last house before dinner. Our Realtor had listed her home, and we followed her down the long driveway.

Nick climbed out of the car and started toward a yellow lab resting on the porch. My mom grabbed his hand.

"It's okay." The Realtor waved Mom off. "He's friendly. He won't bite."

Nick tugged away from Mom, rushed up the stairs, and stuck his face close to the dog's nose. The dog growled and snapped. My brother screamed. Blood oozed through his tiny fingers. My dad scooped him up and carried him into the house. My parents dabbed wet towels against his wounds and thought he needed stitches around his eye.

About 30 minutes later, Betsy and I sat in an Arkansas emergency room with an apologetic Realtor. We all felt bad.

All eyes went to my mom when she stepped through the door. She motioned to me. "Jake, he wants you."

I followed her into the room where Nick lay on a gurney. My little brother smiled and stretched out his arms.

My mom patted my back. "He wouldn't stop crying until I agreed to get you."

I leaned close and whispered in his ear. "With stitches, you're going to be the toughest new guy in town."

Nick giggled and hugged my neck.

I looked up at the physician who waited, ready with a needle. "Doctor, you should see what he did to the other guy."

Calmed and confident now, Nick smiled a toothless grin at the doctor while I held his hand and encouraged him to be brave and not move. The doctor numbed the wounded area and stitched around his eye. My little brother never flinched and the doctor praised his bravery.

> *Carry each other's burdens, and in this way you will fulfill the law of Christ (Galatians 6:2).*

In football, the guy carrying the ball into the end zone scores the points. A runner's rushing attempts are also called carries. That day in the ER, standing by Nick's side and cracking jokes, I may have scored points with my parents and the doctor, but what impacted me was how much my little brother looked up to me. From that day forward, I determined to be a good role model and always be there for him.

When the football is handed to the ball carrier, everyone counts on that guy gaining a down or getting into the end zone, and when he does the crowd goes wild. But those who carry another's burden, by helping out a weak or injured brother or sister, make a real difference and score points with God.

When you're on the run and pushing toward your goals, take time to reach out to others and be their hero. The Bible says we should comfort one another and carry each other's burdens. You may never know how much your presence means to someone, even if just cracking a joke during a tense moment or standing by his or her side through a rough patch.

Chain Gang

The officials, also called the chain crew, who man the chains used for marking down and distance.

Dragging myself into the Wisconsin Badgers weight room at 4:45 a.m. during spring workout, I spotted my name on the board next to three others under the title "Group One." I groaned. Group activities didn't mean a fun game of Twister.

Per instructions, players gathered into teams, and we chained ourselves together with weight belts. The coach handed out two sand bags per team—a 100 pound and a 50 pound—and ordered us to climb to the upper deck of Camp Randall Stadium.

Like a real chain gang, there was no chance of escaping this task or unyoking from one another. Sharing the weighty responsibility, we climbed the steep stadium stairs. One team versus the rest until each team quit because they couldn't go on. The last team standing would be the champion.

> *Accept the one whose faith is weak, without quarreling over disputable matters. One person's faith allows them to eat anything, but another, whose faith is weak, eats only vegetables. The one who eats everything must not treat with contempt the one who does not, and the one who does not eat everything must not judge the one who does, for God has accepted them. Who are you to judge someone else's servant? To their own master, servants stand or fall. And they will stand, for the Lord is able to make them stand (Romans 14:1-4).*

Linked together as a team with one goal, we soon realized we were only as strong as our weakest link. But did we condemn the weaker member? That wouldn't serve any purpose. Instead, the stronger guys responded by carrying more weight than the weaker teammate. Encouragement was key in reaching the top of the stadium, standing as one.

Sometimes one person on your team may not be as strong as another. Strengths usually differ. Likewise, in an encounter with another, someone may have a different set of beliefs or ideas. To accomplish any goal, embracing the strengths and weaknesses of each member and compensating where necessary are the best ways to make it to the top.

Challenge

During the game, coaches can challenge an official's call. The play is then reviewed in slow motion and at various angles to determine whether the official made the correct call or if the coach is correct in challenging the official's call.

I've tackled many challenges in my lifetime. The most satisfying ones were food related. Like the 2-pound burger at Fuddruckers that I had to devour in 15 minutes. Shattered it in 5 minutes and 46 seconds! Or the Blazing Challenge at Buffalo Wild Wings: eat 12 blazing wings in 5 minutes. Killed it in 57 seconds! Quaker Steak and Lube's all-you-can-eat wings in one sitting? I may still hold the record in Madison, Wisconsin, for scarfing down 78. I'll never forget when 6 linemen and I went to a sushi restaurant during the time of the 2011 Rose Bowl in Pasadena. We didn't exactly take on an eating challenge, but we did get kicked out of the place when the owner ordered, "Go home now. You've eaten eight hundred dollars' worth of sushi."

Test me, Lord, and try me, examine my heart and my mind;
for I have always been mindful of your unfailing love and
have lived in reliance on your faithfulness (Psalm 26:2-3).

Not all challenges are like food ones. Some are bad ideas that bite you back later, like the blazing wing challenge. I sure paid for that one the next day.

A challenge can also come from a loved one in the form of a question about your lifestyle, or a doubt about one of your choices or decisions, like the challenge to an official's call. Your conscience may also challenge you, making you reconsider your actions or options. Could be God challenging you to live a Christian life. I get those a lot. For me, God's challenges are more difficult than any food dares.

Are you living a weekend lifestyle that doesn't honor God? Afraid of failure and not answering His call for your life? Making a decision that raises concern from loved ones?

If you want to take on a challenge that you'll never regret, pray the verses from the psalm above. Ask God to test you and examine your heart and mind. Because He loves you, He will show you what to change in your life. Are you tough enough to accept that challenge?

Cheerleader

An athlete who performs routines on the sidelines that involve tumbling, dancing, jumping, and executing stunts to inspire fans to cheer for their team.

At a play-off game with the Chargers, goose bumps ran down my arms as I rushed through the smoke-filled tunnel onto the field. The energy and voices of 70,000 screaming fans can turn even a veteran player's determined squint into the wide eyes of a child on Christmas morning.

While the cheerleaders performed and urged on the crowd, running back Danny Woodhead turned to me. "Can you believe we get to do this?"

> *When he opened the seventh seal, there was silence in heaven for about half an hour. And I saw the seven angels who stand before God, and seven trumpets were given to them. Another angel, who had a golden censer, came and stood at the altar. He was given much incense to offer, with the prayers of all God's people, on the golden altar that is before the throne. The smoke of the incense, together with the prayers of God's people, went up before God from the angel's hand. Then the angel took the censer, filled it with fire from the altar, and hurled it on the earth; and there came peals of thunder, rumblings, flashes of lightning and an earthquake (Revelation 8:1-5).*

This scene in heaven from the book of Revelation sounds like the field before the game—the calm before the storm and then the smoke of incense, peals of thunder, rumbling from the crowd, and flashes of light. But this vivid image from heaven is greater and much more profound, for sure like nothing Danny or I have yet to see.

I'm humbled when fans and cheerleaders yell their hearts out for the team. How much more amazing when saints, angels, and even loved ones who have passed on pray and cheer for us before the throne of God.

Psalm 91:11 says, "He will command his angels concerning you to guard you in all your ways." Angels are assigned to watch over us. The Bible tells us God sends them to earth as messengers and caretakers. They are our cheerleaders who go before God, along with the saints, whom the Bible names as intercessors before Him.

In pursuing your dreams, you may not have 70,000 fans cheering in the stands, yet in heaven a host of angels, saints, and loved ones cheer you on before God. That's pretty cool. And don't be afraid to ask others to pray for you on earth. Those prayers from our earthly cheerleaders, like smoke, travel upward and reach God, who wants you to win.

Clipping

A penalty given as a result of an offensive player
blocking a defensive player from behind, usually at or
below the waist. The penalty is assessed 15 yards from
the previous line of scrimmage. Clipping is a penalty
created to ensure a player's safety, due to the dangerous
nature of blocks from behind on unaware players.

In high school I wore a special rib protector called a "quarterback flap
jacket." Playing wide receiver, I was always getting de-cleated (tackled hard enough to get knocked out of your cleats). Coaches on opposing teams pointed to me as the guy to take out of the game. I was marked as the means to opponents' career plays, vulnerable to being clipped.

During my freshman year at the University of Wisconsin, I ran into Chris Marsh again, a guy who had once targeted me in high school football. On the wall in his den—his family's football shrine room—was a blown-up picture of him bent down in a linebacker stance trying to explode through a hit. Above him, in the picture, I'm reaching for the ball.

"Good thing that picture was snapped before I caught the ball and ran for a first down." I slapped him on the back.

"Nah, pretty sure I made that tackle."

"Nah, pretty sure you didn't."

To this day, we each stick to our own version of what really happened. Pretty sure I'm right.

Be alert and of sober mind. Your enemy the devil prowls
around like a roaring lion looking for someone to devour.
Resist him, standing firm in the faith, because you know

*that the family of believers throughout the world is under-
going the same kind of sufferings (1 Peter 5:8-9).*

Typically, clipping is called when an offensive player throws himself
at the back of an opposing player, particularly if contact is made below
the waist. Getting hit on the field unexpectedly can be disabling. Not
only do players need to be alert, they also have to put on extra armor,
like that flap jacket I had to wear, along with my pads and helmet.

Even though Chris was coached to take me out in high school, he's
a great friend now. The devil, who is never our friend, wants to clip us
on the field of faith and take us out spiritually.

Knowing I was a target in high school, I wore that quarterback
flap jacket for protection. As Christians, we are targets. Are you protected? Focused on God? Are you praying and attending church? Are
you watchful for areas in your life where the devil can clip you?

Coach

The coach is the man in charge, the guy responsible
for the entire team. When the team wins, every
fan boasts that it's because of the coach. When
the team loses, fans and media blame him. He is
motivator, teacher, and leader. The coach sculpts
players into the best athletes they can be in order to
win games. He's also the guy who calls the plays.

Playing for the Texans against Indianapolis in 2013, we were up
by three touchdowns after a few weeks of losses. At halftime, our
morale high, we headed toward the locker room with Coach Gary
Kubiak behind us.

Nearing the tunnel, a collective gasp rose from the stadium. My
teammates and I stopped and turned. Our leader had fallen onto the
ground! Medical staff rushed to his side and officials cleared the crowd
away from the scene. An ambulance soon hauled him away. Without
the rock that held us all together, without our leader and play caller, we
didn't score again and lost that game.

Later, we discovered our head coach had a ministroke. Already dealing with a losing season, the team's morale couldn't get much lower.
Then, more bad news. Coach Kubiak was let go. The one man in the
organization who was loved by all, the one we trusted and respected,
was gone. I'd never seen lower spirits in any team or group of people.
The Texans didn't win another game that season.

> *Then the LORD said to him, "This is the land I promised on
> oath to Abraham, Isaac and Jacob when I said, 'I will give it
> to your descendants.' I have let you see it with your eyes, but
> you will not cross over into it." And Moses the servant of the
> LORD died there in Moab, as the LORD had said.*

Moses—the leader of the Israelites for 40 years—was not allowed to take the people into the Promised Land because he disobeyed God.

When Coach Kubiak was with the Texans, he was a well-loved coach—like Moses was for the Israelites—always taking care of the team and putting players' interests first. Like Coach and Moses, even beloved leaders can fall or fail unexpectedly. Either way, the team suffers. Our hearts went out to the revered man, but we also worried about what would happen to us. Who would lead us?

Has someone you admired fallen, failed, or suddenly disappeared from your life? That makes for tough times. You wonder if you'll pull through. After Coach Kubiak was fired, Wade Phillips, defensive coordinator, was named as the interim coach that 2013 season and the remainder of a shaky team ambled through a losing season.

God sent Joshua to lead the Israelites into the Promised Land. Later, in the fullness of time, God sent Jesus, His Son, to earth—as God and human—to live among us and be our Savior. When we're in need of a leader, we don't have to worry. God always sends someone. We must regroup and move on but never give up.

Cut

You're removed from a football team when you're
cut. The word also refers to a block below the
waist when trying to literally flip the defender
over and cut their legs out from under them.

In preseason with the New Orleans Saints, on cut day my nerves were shot. Though I was confident I'd performed well and earned my spot on the team, some factors were beyond my control. In the NFL, a guy in your position can be judged as better. Sometimes the team doesn't have a spot for you anymore, as the number of players must be cut from 80-plus down to the 53-man roster. It's a sad time, and many of the friends you made during the early practice sessions in August can soon be out of your life.

Even if you make the team, injuries or illness can take you out of the game quickly and often permanently. Professional football is one of the toughest jobs to keep, and on cut day I wondered if I'd be turning in my Saints' playbook.

> *Do not be anxious about anything, but in every situation,*
> *by prayer and petition, with thanksgiving, present your*
> *requests to God. And the peace of God, which transcends*
> *all understanding, will guard your hearts and your minds*
> *in Christ Jesus (Philippians 4:6-7).*

I had lasted through the camps, played a couple of preseason games, and then got cut just before the first game of the regular season. The Saints didn't want to risk developing a younger player like myself and brought in a veteran tight end. Later that season, I was picked up by the Houston Texans, a team where my talents were better utilized.

I love playing the game, but worry? No point. Paul's letter to the Philippians says it all. Don't be anxious. Pray. God knows where you need to be and will give you a sense of peace in all of the ups and downs of life that leave you feeling as if you've been flipped onto your backside.

If you feel as if your legs have been cut from underneath you, get back up. If a door closes, don't spend time staring at it. Be at peace and look for the open one. It'll be there. Then, walk through it into the next phase of your life.

Dancing

When a player shifts his body horizontally and
quickly moves his feet to get the defender off
balance so to avoid contact and gain extra yards.

My good friend Brittany slammed her locker shut. Tears brimmed above her bottom lashes. Her dance partner had backed out a couple of weeks before West Side Studio's city-wide *Nutcracker* performance.

High school seniors now, we'd been good friends since the fifth grade. She'd do anything for me. Though she didn't ask, her look said, *Jake, could you please take his place?*

I offered to be her partner if she couldn't find anyone else, and then I wondered what I'd gotten myself into when no one came forward.

Leaping around on stage with a bunch of people half my size? It would be a comedy, not a ballet. I was sure there was no way size 15 ballet slippers and tights that would fit me even existed. Turns out they did.

Football always came natural, a sport I excelled at, so I figured my sure-footedness and athletic ability would prove ballet dancing wasn't out of my league. My competitive nature fueled me, and I strived to be the best. Each day after football practice, I worked hard to make sure my lack of skill didn't prevent Brittany from shining.

Opening night was Brittany's game day. Backstage, she stood poised and prepared. My confidence disappeared. What if I forgot my routine? Tripped? Landed like an oak tree on the stage? Butterflies fluttered to their own choreography inside my gut. Brittany had been doing this her entire life, but I was as nervous as a freshman during kickoff at the first game of the season.

> *There is a time for everything, and a season for every activity under the heavens: a time to be born and a time to die, a*

> *time to plant and a time to uproot, a time to kill and a time*
> *to heal, a time to tear down and a time to build, a time to*
> *weep and a time to laugh, a time to mourn and a time to*
> *dance (Ecclesiastes 3:1-4).*

The night of the *Nutcracker*, my younger brother and sister sat in the audience, probably dying of laughter. I could've sworn I heard snickering. I'd already endured a ton of ribbing from teammates and expected a lot more come Monday. Nevertheless, I stepped on stage to perform my small role. To the classical music of Tchaikovsky, Brittany and I danced. With the spotlight on us, my moves were as smooth as my Friday night performances under stadium lights. Holding hands at the final bow, our smiles stretched ear to ear. I didn't hear one laugh in the audience, only applause and cheers.

Sometimes we're caught off guard and asked to do something we may not want to do, something outside our comfort zone—a favor, a challenge. We could be mocked or ridiculed. Or maybe we'll doubt ourselves, but we can't let fear rule. Sometimes in life, we have to dance.

Defensive End

A defensive player who lines up at the end of
the defensive line. He wants to disrupt the play
and cause as much trouble for the blocker as
possible. His job is to contain the running back on
running plays and not let him get to the outside.
He also rushes the quarterback on passing plays,
keeping him inside and hopefully sacking him.

After graduating early from high school, I carefully listened to the quarterback during my first play in college spring ball. My mind was on the very basics of football: alignment, assignment, and where to stand in the huddle. The quarterback broke the huddle and I ran to the line, meeting the confident eyes of a defensive end—6-foot-6, 260-pound Matt Shaughnessy.

I was seventeen, a true freshman, and he was a 23-year-old fifth-year senior, a third-round draft pick. Huge difference between the two of us. Impressing the coach was not on my mind. Survival was. "Oh, Jesus," I said. I wasn't cursing. I was praying for help.

Is anyone among you in trouble? Let them pray (James 5:13).

That day Matt came off the ball so fast. *Bam!* Next thing I knew, I was flat on my back, thrown to the ground. I got up and limped back to the huddle.

Four years later…standing on the sidelines in my first NFL game, bouncing on my toes, waiting for my chance to go in, one of the tight ends went down. My time to shine! Where do I stand? Who do I have? I look up and meet the same eyes I met on my first play in college football.

Matt Shaughnessy!

Now a third-year NFL veteran, he is the other team's defensive end.

The ball snaps. I'm now pass-blocking him, thinking I'm doing an awesome job, pushing past the pile and securing the edge. Then Matt rips under my right hand and forces it under his face mask. My first play in the NFL resulted in a penalty. He got the better of me again.

Troubles can reappear even when we are doing our best. We are good intentioned, charging forward toward our goal, and then *bam!* We get hit. Maybe it's not in the form of a half-ton linebacker (though it may feel like it).

A defensive end is looking to mess you up. Life is like that too. Sometimes you think you are doing an excellent job, and then you get bull-rushed by the defensive end, and he blows by you and gets the better of you. Do your best, pick yourself up, limp back to the huddle, and when you're in trouble, pray! Whatever the outcome, get up and carry on, doing what you are called to do.

Disguise Coverage

When the defense adjusts its coverage to trick the
offense. The defense will align in one form of coverage
and shift to another after the ball is snapped to prevent
the offense from recognizing which type of coverage
they are using. They usually switch their alignment
and make you think they are going to do one thing
when they are actually attempting something else.

When I was five, my mom took my little sister and brother and me
to a pumpkin patch. We met a crowd of kids talking to a pumpkin. Well, not exactly a pumpkin, but a four-foot round orange object
with dark mesh covering the eye and mouth openings.

The scene did not sit right with me. I wanted to understand this
odd pumpkin being, but I'd given up believing in the Easter Bunny
at age four because I couldn't fathom the idea of a six-foot-tall bunny
who filled kids' baskets with candy once a year. Rabbits don't get that
big. And talking pumpkins? No way. Didn't fly with me.

That autumn day at the pumpkin patch, I took a step closer to Mr.
Pumpkin. "You're not really a pumpkin."

Mr. Pumpkin chuckled low. "Why, sure I am, little boy."

I asked him a lot of questions, like if he was a very short guy, or a
kid that could fit inside the pumpkin, or a guy standing somewhere
else and talking into a microphone. While I attempted to solve the
pumpkin patch mystery, my mom tugged me away from the murmuring crowd. She frowned and said parents were upset because their kids
actually believed in that orange dude. Apparently, I'd ruined the day
for a few innocent, trusting children.

False messiahs and false prophets will appear and perform
great signs and wonders to deceive, if possible, even the elect
(Matthew 24:24).

From a young age I was a straight shooter who didn't put up with nonsense. I didn't like to be tricked even in fun. Though Mr. Pumpkin probably hadn't engineered an evil plan to lead kids down a bad path, I felt it was better to recognize what was real and what wasn't so I didn't get tricked. That was my take back then. It still is today.

In football, the disguise coverage can trick us and throw us off. You have to be on your toes and aware. The same applies to all life situations. The wise recognize liars, false prophets, and false teachings. Maintaining spiritual insight keeps us on track with God's plan.

Confused? Got questions? When in doubt, ask God, seek His wisdom, study Scripture, and talk to your pastor or a trusted Christian friend. But don't be tricked, even if the rest of the crowd is lured into false teaching.

Double Team

A defensive scheme that uses two defenders to cover and be responsible for one player. It can be a combination of any two defensive players or offensive players working with each other against one of the opponents. They work together to help each other.

On the first day of fourth grade in Arkansas, during art class, I stared at the blank sheet of paper clipped onto the easel. The teacher had given the class the option to either choose a partner and draw a scene or work alone. I didn't know anyone in the class. I had been in this situation before. I left all of my friends to start over at a new school. I had attended three different kindergartens and had moved almost once a year since.

Quickly making new friends was key to survival at a new school. I glanced around the room. In the corner, another kid—big like me—stood alone before his easel. I approached him and checked out his work. He'd already sketched out a car, my favorite thing to draw.

He looked up. "Hi. I'm Bobby. Want to join me?"

"Sure."

Like me, Bobby was a new kid. We stared at the blank paper and immediately our imaginations kicked in.

"Let's create a city," Bobby said.

"I can draw cars."

While designing and creating our city, our quickly formed friendship deepened.

In middle school, Bobby and I were an unstoppable duo on the football field—often working in pair to complement the team. Classmates called us the Bobby-Jake show. He played running back on offense and linebacker on defense. I played tight end and defensive end. Every time I ran the ball, he rushed. Every time he threw the ball, I caught it. Land and air.

Many times in sports, especially in football, a team needs to be broken down and positions need to work together in double teams. As the linebacker who played behind me, we spent many hours practicing our blitz combinations. When Bobby went inside, I went outside, and vice versa. A team within a team.

Offense was much the same. When Bobby blocked the defensive end in front of me, I helped set up his block by punching the shoulder of the defensive end just enough to stand him up and slow him down, so Bobby could complete the block before I moved on to the linebacker.

My first game on an NFL roster, Bobby, working in Dallas, came down to Houston to watch me play, and then he drove five hours back home after the game. No matter what life has thrown at us, we've been double-teaming since we created our make-believe city in the fourth grade.

> As soon as he had finished speaking to Saul, the soul of Jonathan was knit to the soul of David, and Jonathan loved him as his own soul. And Saul took him that day and would not let him return to his father's house. Then Jonathan made a covenant with David, because he loved him as his own soul. And Jonathan stripped himself of the robe that was on him and gave it to David, and his armor, and even his sword and his bow and his belt (1 Samuel 18:1-4 ESV).

Jonathan was King Saul's oldest son and should have been the rightful heir to the throne. The king grew jealous of David and wanted him dead, but Jonathan put his friendship with David ahead of his role as son to his father. Like the offensive line defends the quarterback, Jonathan risked everything to defend his friend.

Friends come and go, but Bobby has stuck by me like a brother as Jonathan did for David. And Jesus, our brother through our relationship with God, our Father, is a friend who "sticks closer than a brother" (Proverbs 18:24). He's always right there to double team with us through every arena in our life.

Draft Choice

The order in which a college NFL prospect is chosen.
Each of the 32 NFL teams has picks through all 7
rounds of the annual draft. The order of the team's draft
pick is based on the team's record from the previous
year. Teams with the most losses get first picks. Teams
also may trade picks during the draft process.

I wasn't a draft pick. I went into the NFL as an undrafted free agent. I learned right away that even for those drafted, there are no guarantees. The NFL isn't just a sport; it's big business. During my first rookie minicamp, I overheard coaches talking about a guy who didn't make the flight to the camp. His reason could have been something beyond his ability to control, like a canceled flight, but the conversation didn't even go that far. One coach said, "If he's not responsible enough to get on the flight, we're good. Bring in the next guy."

Another player drove nine hours from his home in Texas to New Orleans, only to be cut and sent home minutes after walking in the door. No reason given. He turned around and drove back home. Ouch!

> *Are not five sparrows sold for two pennies? Yet not one of them is forgotten by God. Indeed, the very hairs of your head are all numbered. Don't be afraid; you are worth more than many sparrows (Luke 12:6-7).*

The NFL determines your worth as a player, but only God knows your true worth. Players work long and hard through pain and suffering, injuries, and pushing themselves further than they imagined going—then poof! A dream is gone. That kind of treatment can really mess with one's self-worth. Getting cut can be deemed a failure, the loss of a lifetime goal.

Thankfully, as Christians our worth is not determined by mistakes we've made, either accidentally or by stupid stuff we've purposely done. Neither is it determined by what anyone else thinks. Our worth is determined by what Jesus Christ has already done. Willingly dying on the cross, He paid the ultimate penalty for our sins. He loves us that much. If we are worth dying for, how can anything that happens in our life lower our worth? God has drafted all who believe in His Son, and His is a draft that doesn't allow for cuts.

Encroachment

A penalty called when a defensive player
crosses the neutral zone before the ball is
snapped, resulting in a five-yard penalty.

In the fourth grade, as I was hanging out on the sidewalk at Reagan
Elementary and bouncing a small stone off a basketball, a classmate
encroached upon my territory. He stepped into my circle of play, and
in an attempt to outdo me took a rock and smashed it against the ball.
The rock bounced off the ball and then against the glass door, shatter-
ing it into a million pieces. Standing near a pile of broken glass with a
stone still in my hand, I was doomed. Teachers surrounded us within
seconds.

> *Be always on the watch, and pray that you may be able to
> escape all that is about to happen, and that you may be able
> to stand before the Son of Man (Luke 21:36).*

An encroachment on the field is a violation. Once, during a game
with the Texans, the defensive end came across the line early and hit
me before I could move. The hit caught me off guard, and it took a few
seconds before I could refocus. He was penalized, but I paid the price.

In life, encroachment means someone or something has entered
into your personal space, like that kid at Reagan Elementary. When he
picked up the stone, I should have leaped to my feet and left the potential disaster zone. I knew what was going to happen. I could see the
outcome before he threw the stone. As a result, I was penalized along
with that kid, gaining me my very first in-school suspension. Thankfully, my parents accepted my side of the story, but the principal wasn't
so understanding. "Guilt by association," he said. My parents had to
help pay to replace the door.

You always have to be alert and watch out for trouble because trouble can take you out of the game. Have you had encroachment of some sort in your life? Maybe a troublemaker is entering into your playing field. Be aware. Be alert. Having stood firm in your faith, throughout all of life's situations, you will be able to stand with confidence before Jesus on judgment day.

Excessive Celebrating

A player's touchdown celebration that exceeds
a normal, personal expression and taunts
opposing players, is overdone, or takes
away from the good nature of the sport.

Packing for the last preseason game against the Cowboys, I didn't have enough clean underwear. I shuffled through my dresser drawers and only found Spiderman whitey-tighties. One of my college roommates had bought a package as a joke and we all took a pair. I tossed them in my bag. They would have to do.

That Sunday we beat the Cowboys! I managed to avoid excessive celebration on the field, but postgame I was stoked. In the locker room, the Texans' general manager walked through the door and caught me in a victory dance in my Spiderman underwear. He looked me over and shook his head. "I don't even know what to say to that."

> *Wearing a linen ephod, David was dancing before the LORD with all his might, while he and all Israel were bringing up the ark of the LORD with shouts and the sound of trumpets. As the ark of the LORD was entering the City of David, Michal daughter of Saul watched from a window. And when she saw King David leaping and dancing before the LORD, she despised him in her heart (2 Samuel 6:14-16).*

When David's wife went ballistic, he responded, "I will celebrate before the LORD. I will become even more undignified than this, and I will be humiliated in my own eyes" (2 Samuel 6:21-22). David was living large in the moment, praising and worshipping the Lord. He wasn't worried about what he was or wasn't wearing, and he didn't appreciate his wife's attitude.

There is nothing wrong with praising the Lord and celebrating life and the victories God gives us. I'm not saying we should dance in our underwear at the wrong time or in an inappropriate place. Rules and social norms must be followed, of course. Excessive celebration will get you a penalty on the field. But otherwise, don't worry about how you look. When the situation calls for it, dance.

Formation *257828*

The team alignment, offensively and defensively,
of the 11 members on the field for each team.
Offensively, 7 players must line up on the line of
scrimmage, with 2 of them on each side eligible
receivers. The rest line up either as running backs or
receivers off the line of scrimmage. This is done to
try to confuse the defensive formation, who can put
their 11 players anywhere they like but usually will
base their alignment on what the offense does.

Taller than my teacher, tiny Mrs. Botinni, I was assigned as the second grade line leader—the student responsible to lead classmates to the gym, library, lunch, recess, or any activities outside of the classroom. When she called for us to line up, I would assume my position in front and everyone else would stand behind me. This duty set me up as someone to look up to, literally.

> *Just as a body, though one, has many parts, but all its many parts form one body, so it is with Christ. For we were all baptized by one Spirit so as to form one body—whether Jews or Gentiles, slave or free—and we were all given the one Spirit to drink. Even so the body is not made up of one part but of many (1 Corinthians 12:12-14).*

Formation in football is all about the alignment of the players, set and controlled by the coach who is called the team's offensive or defensive coordinator. He's in charge of making sure all of the players are in the right formation and executing their prescribed assignments—the leaders behind the scene.

Offensively each player must execute his responsibility from his formation. Defense is responsible to adjust to the offense and cover their assignment and opposing player.

As a second grade line leader, my duty was to get classmates from one place to the next, often without Mrs. Botinni. If a student got out of formation or acted up, I'd stop the line and restore order. Sometimes I'd set the formation offensively, making sure classmates were in their assigned place and adjusting them defensively if they were not. When each person followed the formation, our group arrived at our destination.

The coordinator is one of many parts of a football team. While he is responsible for the formation and assignments, each player must carry out his individual role. When everyone does their job responsibly, the team wins.

The apostle Paul tells the Corinthians that they are all part of one body in Christ. Wherever God places us in life's formation—a leader or a follower—the body of Christ benefits when we maintain responsible order.

Fourth and Goal

The last play in the red zone when teams
must make the decision to either kick a
field goal or try for the touchdown.

Prior to my senior year in college, my head coach, Bret Bielema, was
quoted saying, "For a receiving corps that features big-time playmaker Nick Toon and 'Mr. Reliable' Jake Byrne at tight end, it's like
Christmas in June for the Badgers."

After a challenging start in college football, I was honored that my
coach called me "Mr. Reliable."

That season, on a fourth and goal from the one yard line, one play
came down to that one important block I had to make on the defensive end. As the quarterback came to the line, I focused on the down
block I needed to make so our fullback could come off the edge and
clean up a linebacker to free running back Montee Ball, another excep-
tional player for the Badgers.

I dug in, gritted my teeth, and on first sound drew upon all my
strength, experience, and discipline to make the block.

> *It is required that those who have been given a trust must
> prove faithful (1 Corinthians 4:2).*

Sometimes in life it comes down to that big decision you need to
make at fourth and goal. *Will I get the touchdown or settle for just a field
goal? Will I get stopped altogether?* Fourth and goal is the last chance you
have, and that's that difference from scoring a touchdown or getting a
field goal. When you're trying to move the ball six inches, it's you versus the defensive lineman across from you. Little things matter, like
who is going to be more disciplined? Who is going to get the job done?
You or him?

Being reliable is making sure I'm never the weak link in any situation—as a brother, a son, a football player, or a Christian.

How responsible are you with what you are given? Are you the person who, when asked to do a job, can be counted on to get it done and get it done right? Don't settle for just a field goal in life. Make the push for the last six inches and score a touchdown. Faithfulness, hard work, and dedication will gain the trust of others and take you further down the field.

Franchise Tag

When an NFL organization tags an elite player as a
franchise player, he will be paid the average salary
of the top five players at his position for that year.

On a nutrition website, I saw that my name was on a list of famous people with diabetes. It was the first time I had ever seen my name and the word "famous" together. My skills haven't brought me near the status of a franchise player, but having diabetes has brought attention to me as an NFL player and on a list with Halle Berry and Tom Hanks. The list of professional athletes with diabetes is very small. Not long after that, I got the little blue check after my name on Twitter. Verified because of football.

> His disciples asked him, "Rabbi, who sinned, this man or
> his parents, that he was born blind?" "Neither this man nor
> his parents sinned," said Jesus, "but this happened so that
> the works of God might be displayed in him. As long as it
> is day, we must do the works of him who sent me. Night is
> coming, when no one can work. While I am in the world, I
> am the light of the world" (John 9:2-5).

When Jesus walked the earth, people thought having a disability or a disease was the result of sin. But Jesus clears this up. A blind guy—a nobody on the street—became an overnight sensation, famous when healed by Jesus and featured in the Bible, the bestselling book in the world. We still talk about that guy more than 2000 years later.

Sometimes God can use your disability, disease, or challenge to make you a key player in whatever He has called you to do. Maybe that thing that you have to deal with—that thorn in your flesh—is something God is allowing you to have so His light can shine more in you and show others more about Him.

Having diabetes is a real challenge, especially in playing professional sports. But because of diabetes, doors have opened for me. I've met some great people and have had some amazing experiences. What problem, illness, or issue do you have that God can turn from bothersome to blessing?

Fumble

When an offensive player loses possession of the ball.

In the sixth grade, while playing basketball against a rival team, I got flustered and turned around on a rebound. The member of the other team shot a free throw. He missed and I jumped up and tipped the ball right in...the wrong basket, scoring two points for the other team. My ears lit up in shame when I heard the crowd laugh and point. Unlike football, where you can hide under your helmet after a fumble, basketball is just you in a sleeveless shirt with your name on your back.

> *To the roots of the mountains I sank down; the earth beneath barred me in forever. But you, LORD my God, brought my life up from the pit (Jonah 2:6).*

In football I could always hold on to the ball and never ran the wrong way. But fumbles happen often in the sport, and if not recovered, they can cause the loss of ball possession and possibly the loss of a game.

Fumbles happen in life too. The Bible is full of people who really messed up. Even Peter denied Christ three times after swearing that he wouldn't. When Jesus was resurrected, He asked Peter three times if he loved Him. Three times Peter said yes, and the Lord's forgiveness restored him.

When we're recovering from a spiritual fumble, we must realize everyone does stupid stuff. No one is exempt. An occasional misstep doesn't brand us as stupid—it makes us real. God loves us regardless of our mishaps. After a fumble, do as any good football player would. Fight to recover what you lost, get back into the game, and let the Creator turn your loss into a gain. With Him, in spite of our fumbles we can rise to great heights.

Game Plan

A team's strategy against their opponent of the week.

When I arrived at the University of Wisconsin at age 17, I was fifth string with three future NFL tight ends in front of me: Lance Kendricks, Garrett Graham, and Travis Beckum. I played the game but had no game plan for a future in football. For two years I'd call home and complain about how much I hated football and was ready to be done with it.

No way could I compete with the other tight ends' level of talent. Travis was an All-American, the best tight end in the country. Those other guys had their eye on the NFL, but getting a free education was about as far as it went for me. So I did what I had to do but not much more.

Then my tight end coach, Joe Rudolph, said something that made sense. "Fight for your own limitation."

A shift occurred in my mind. Watching the older guys, I told myself, *Stop making excuses. If you want what they have, work for it.*

That decision propelled me into devising a game plan for success on the field. Off season, I put extra time in the weight room, lifting until they kicked me out—first one to get there, last to leave. I worked like a starving animal in search of its prey to earn a starting spot. Instead of thinking that I'd never be as good as them, I began to think about what I could learn from them. So I followed their example, studied what they did that got results, and worked hard. I also considered what I did best and built upon it.

I matured a bit and seriously focused on goals. And every moment of working toward my goals was incredibly difficult. It's never easy to push yourself, but I had a game plan for success.

At the end of that season, the strength coach gave me the Badger

Power Award for the player most committed in the weight room. The next season, after Travis and Garrett left, I earned a starting spot!

The heart of the discerning acquires knowledge, for the ears of the wise seek it out (Proverbs 18:15).

You can't be the best just because you want it. You have to make a game plan and work toward your goal. Same goes for any area of your life, even your spiritual life. Do you have a game plan for getting to heaven? Are you following Christ? Is there a strong Christian person you admire? Listen to them, find out what they are doing right, and work out your game plan for being a successful Christian. There's no better feeling than the result of hard work.

Gap

A gap is the space between offensive linemen
that needs to be accounted for by the defensive
player. Gap "A" is between the center and
guard, "B" is between the guard and tackle,
and "C" is between the tackle and guard.

In high school there was a guy on my football team who also had type 1 diabetes. His blood sugar levels could hit 400 to 500 (normal is 70 to 120), and he often missed practice. Diabetes was giving him a terrible time. Everyone is different and I didn't know about his struggles, but I wondered how well he handled his diabetes with diet and exercise. How did he prepare himself—mentally and physically—not only for practice but in everyday life? Was he covering all the gaps? While I felt sorry for him, his situation scared me because I never wanted to allow myself to become unstable with my disease.

There is one God and one mediator between God and mankind, the man Christ Jesus (1 Timothy 2:5).

On defense, coaches insist players be "gap sound." Each person must do his job and not leave a gap. He must be disciplined.

Managing diabetes must also be a consistent discipline process. You can't have gaps. You can't avoid checking blood sugar. While there is no cure for type 1 diabetes, there are things you can do to control the disease.

Sometimes those with type 1 diabetes, especially kids, go to bed while levels are still fluctuating. You have to cover that gap. I make it a point to get stable an hour or so before I go to bed, practice, or go out with friends at night so I don't have those lows. This discipline has worked for me. I have to keep on top of diabetes. Diet and exercise are important factors. Not checking blood sugar levels isn't an option.

Gaps are holes. Empty spaces. The gap between heaven and earth, created by sin, was filled by Jesus—God becoming man. The filling of this gap gave us eternal life. Have you embraced Jesus as your Savior and filled this gap? Are you gap sound in your life? Disciplined? Do you have gaps that need to be filled? If so, what's keeping you from being on top of your game?

Hail Mary

An offensive play where the quarterback throws the
ball as high and far as he can, hoping someone on
his team can make a miracle catch. A Hail Mary is
generally used on the last play of the half or at the
end of the game when a team is out of field goal
range and has just enough time for one more play.

I read that out of 100,000 high school seniors playing football, only 9,000 become college players, and of those, only 215 become NFL players. That's about two-tenths of a percent. And out of the two-tenths, far as I knew, I was the only type 1 diabetic rookie going into the 2012 football draft. Even with the odds against me, all I wanted was a chance to get on to a team. I knelt before God in prayer and threw a Hail Mary up to heaven.

> *In the sixth month the angel Gabriel was sent from God unto a city of Galilee, named Nazareth, to a virgin espoused to a man whose name was Joseph, of the house of David; and the virgin's name was Mary. And the angel came in unto her, and said, Hail, thou that art highly favored, the Lord is with thee: blessed art thou among women (Luke 1:26-28 KJV).*

What were the chances of a young virgin of Nazareth giving birth to the Savior of the world? Did Mary ever whisper a prayer to God, giving her will over to Him? I'm not sure, but when God sent the angel Gabriel to her, she said yes, which led to a victory, a delivery of a Savior into a world desperately needing one.

In football, a Hail Mary is thrown in hope that something good will come from a last-ditch effort. It's an act of total surrender, leaving it to God that the football lands in the right player's hands. Everything could go wrong. Its outcome is a victory or a loss. But with God, there is no defeat. If we accept the gift of Jesus, we receive salvation and eternal life. A win!

My chances at getting drafted by the NFL in 2012? Slim to none. But on draft day, after all the players were chosen, I got a call that landed me—a kid with diabetes—into the career of my dreams. I ended up as a free agent, signing with the New Orleans Saints.

Have you ever lost hope? Wondered where you were going? What you were going to do? Do you hold a dream in your heart that you desire so much you can taste it? Offer up a solid, deep prayer from your heart. God sent a Savior into the world, a baby boy born to a virgin. He can turn your dreams—however impossible they may seem—into reality. Sometimes it takes a willing, obedient heart like Mary's for the miracle to happen.

Halfback Pass

A play intended to fool the defensive players
into thinking the offensive player is running, not
throwing the ball. The running back takes the
ball and starts to run. He then stops his run and
throws the ball to an open receiver down the field
in hopes of a big result, like a touchdown.

In college, while starting as a tight end for the Wisconsin Badgers,
Joey Balistrieri, a fourth-grader with type 1 diabetes, contacted me
through social media. According to Joey, the disease wasn't his biggest
problem. He had to convince his mom he could still play football.

*What you have heard from me in the presence of many wit-
nesses entrust to faithful men who will be able to teach others also (2 Timothy 2:2 ESV).*

Throwing a halfback pass can catch the defense off guard and gain
extra points for the team. It's a high-risk, big-reward play. In short, a
leap of faith. But how sweet and exciting when it works.

Joey worried he'd never see time on the field, but he turned the situation around by searching me out and gathering information to pass
on to his mom, a play that earned him a big reward: a chance to play
football.

His determination and passion for the sport impressed me. He
asked a lot of questions—from how to protect your insulin pump during games to how playing football affected blood sugar levels.

When I was diagnosed, I didn't have mentors. I learned by trial and
error how food, heat, and exercise impacted blood sugar, so I was happy
to help Joey. I sent him pictures to show how I protected my pump
during practice and games. We exchanged email and eventually I spent
time with him and his family.

Now, not only is he a beast of an athlete—killing it on the football field and basketball court too—but he was also named Wisconsin American Diabetes Association Youth Ambassador. He's going full speed ahead in mentoring other kids with diabetes, paying it forward in a big way.

Joey calls me his mentor and friend, but he inspires me and many others. Passing on knowledge benefits the team as well as the body of Christ. We are all gifted with different talents, abilities, and strengths. Sometimes we need to do the unexpected, take a risk for the high reward, and then always be ready to pass along what we've learned to others.

The biggest halfback play is to give our lives to God and serve others. It pays off with the highest reward. Have you learned something in your life that has helped you achieve a goal or gain confidence? Pass it along. Teach others. How sweet and exciting it is when our efforts for God bring about a positive outcome.

Handoff

When one offensive player passes the
ball to another, carefully placing it into his
teammate's hands so not to cause a fumble.

I got this one, Mom."

"If you need me, call. I'll be right there."

"How much trouble can three boys be?" I waved off my mother's worried look and ran across the street to the neighbor's house for my first babysitting job, confident at age 12 that I could handle playing video games for a couple of hours with three little boys.

When the two-year-old ran out the front door, I scooped him up in the driveway, brought him inside, and chained the door. When the two older boys pounded on each other, no problem. I separated them. When the dog's tail knocked over the popcorn bowl, I put all the kids to work picking the popcorn up. I'd handled all of these crises without calling Mom. So far, so good.

I set a new bowl of popcorn on the floor and relaxed next to Jeffrey, who was dominating the video game. Then the toddler took off running. I cornered him and sniffed. "What's that smell?"

"Poopy diaper," Bradley said, not looking away from the TV.

I cringed. "Can it wait until your mom gets home?"

"No." Jeffrey tapped furiously on the game button. "You have to change him right away."

The little guy eyed me and hid behind the chair. I grabbed the phone. "Mom! Help!"

The doorbell rang seconds later.

Two are better than one, because they have a good return
for their labor: If either of them falls down, one can help the

other up. But pity anyone who falls and has no one to help them up (Ecclesiastes 4:9-10).

In football, sometimes the best play is a handoff. The Bible says two are better than one. I thought I could handle three boys for a few hours. What a joke. I tried, but I had my breaking point. I needed to hand off that little guy to my mom. When she came through the door, without hesitation I grabbed the baby and placed him in her hands without causing a fumble. She changed the diaper and even got out the vacuum and took care of the popcorn we missed, which was actually quite a bit.

Don't be too proud to call for help when you need it. Sometimes the right thing to do is to hand off your situation to someone you can trust.

Hash Marks

Hash marks are two rows of lines on a football field
that signify one yard. They are used for marking and
placing the ball on or between the marks, depending
on where the ball was downed during the previous play.

I got in my stance to run my route in practice, ready to start my high school junior year football season, make a name for myself, and earn a football scholarship. My hands shook. Sweat dripped off my face. A sluggish feeling drained me. Something wasn't right.

Diabetes! I knew I ought to take myself out of practice and check my levels, but I didn't want to leave the playing field. I had never let down my team. I had never taken a play off or skipped practice. I was the leader everyone counted on. Now I needed a shoulder to lean on. My weak knees buckled and I fell to the ground. Teammates instantly surrounded me and carried me to the trainer's table.

After I checked my levels and injected insulin, my coach said, "It doesn't pay to be stubborn. You have diabetes, Jake. Don't deny it. Embrace it and take time to take care of yourself. We need you at the top of your game."

Brothers and sisters, I do not consider myself yet to have taken hold of it. But one thing I do: Forgetting what is behind and straining toward what is ahead, I press on toward the goal to win the prize for which God has called me heavenward in Christ Jesus (Philippians 3:13-14).

I wasn't embarrassed by diabetes, but I didn't want to accept that it was affecting me. I quickly learned that being proactive—taking the time and necessary steps to care for myself—was an effective way to fight the disease.

Football is a game of inches. Every inch matters on the way down the field. The numbers on the field mark progress, and the hash marks keep the game centered, just like checking blood sugar levels keeps a diabetic centered. An athlete, a person who is managing diabetes, or anyone can develop their own system of hash marks to chart their progress. Checking my levels often and tracking small, measurable inches toward any goal has turned into long-term benefits for me.

In the letter to the Philippians, the apostle Paul says to press on toward the goal to win the prize. His admonition is encouraging. Even he admits he's not yet taken ahold of it. Whatever your struggle is, consider how you can positively move forward, even by inches, toward your goal. Then as you press on toward the prize, you can celebrate both the journey and the victory.

Hiked

The action in which the ball is handed or
hiked by the center to the quarterback,
holder on a kick attempt, or to the punter.

When I was four years old and living in the hills of West Central Pennsylvania, one Saturday my mom mentioned to my dad that my bike's training wheels needed to be tightened.

"Why are they called training wheels?" I asked.

My dad tousled my hair. "To train you to ride your bike."

I'd heard too many gross discussions about my baby sister's potty training achievements. "I'm trained," I insisted. "Take them off."

"I don't think you're ready." My mom crossed her arms.

If my sister was ready to go without training pants, I could ride my bike without training wheels. I threw a fit and my parents relented. A few minutes later, my dad got his tools and removed the wheels. Then, on the ridge of our sloping, several-acre yard, my mom pushed me while my dad waited below, near the driveway.

Without the training wheels the bike wobbled, but I kept it from falling over. Failure wasn't an option. Part natural sense of balance, part determination, and part fear kept me going. I blew past my dad. Getting the hang of it, I rode all over the yard, up the driveway, and around the house. As I circled the house a second time, my confidence grew and a powerful sense of freedom filled me. I was in control of the bike and I didn't want the ride to stop.

> It is for freedom that Christ has set us free. Stand firm, then,
> and do not let yourselves be burdened again by a yoke of
> slavery (Galatians 5:1).

That childhood memory stuck with me because of the thrilling sense of freedom. Funny, but the day before I thought those little wheels were a permanent part of the bike and had no idea they held me back from speed! What a liberating life moment!

When the ball is snapped in football, the potential for a great play begins. The hope is that the receiver breaks free and runs toward the goal. That same sense of hope is ours when we submit our life plans to God. In doing so, we discover we're not bound by anything keeping us from our goals because with God, all things are possible.

Like that push on the two-wheeler—the power in my legs that kept me pedaling, the thrill of freedom, the wind in my face—a move toward Christ unshackles us from sin and propels us into a new, thrilling life. Freed, we gain an amazing knowledge that nothing can hold us back from our God-ordained dreams and goals.

Holding

*Holding is a penalty that can be called
on either an offensive or defensive player
when they grab the opposing player.*

In fifth grade I played Youth Center Football in Rogers, Arkansas. I was one of the fastest and biggest kids on the team. The coach put me in the game as a running back.

Coolest position.

I was scoring touchdowns and loving football. But the rules contained a weight limit for ball carriers. After a player on defense got a penalty for holding, complaints from the opposing team's coach were brought before my coach. Other kids said they had to hold because of my size. That was the only way they could handle me and get some type of advantage. I was pulled from the game and put on a scale.

One stripe on the helmet meant ten pounds over the limit. The coach slapped two stripes on mine. Taller than I was fat, no way I could lose the weight and stay in that position, so I got moved to offensive lineman. I went from being the hero to protecting the guys who made the big plays. It was a move out of my comfort zone, but for the team I reluctantly accepted the new position.

*I am about to do something new. See, I have already begun!
Do you not see it? (Isaiah 43:19 NLT).*

A comfort zone can be an enemy of your future, a block to success, or a holding penalty that pushes you back, prevents growth, and offers no challenge.

Even though I didn't get to play the position I wanted, I loved football enough to do what it took to stay in the game. If I couldn't be the running back, I was determined to be the best offensive lineman.

Throughout my career, I've been a receiver, fullback, tight end, defensive end, outside linebacker, offensive lineman, offensive tackle, and special teams player. As I look back now, moving out of one specific position—even if reluctantly—benefited me. I became a more versatile player and enjoyed an advantage over others who stayed in one position for their football career.

Sometimes we have to bust out of our comfort zones to become something else for the sake of the team. God can't help if you're unwilling to launch out into something new, and you'll never leave or surpass your current reality. In the game of life, don't let your fear—or anyone else's—hold you back when trying to break out of your comfort zone. Holding is a penalty in football, and it should be in life as well.

Home and Away

For each game, the team from the hosting city
is the home team and the other is the away
team. The Super Bowl is played in a neutral
city determined before the season starts.

S ay cheese!" My roommate's girlfriend held up her iPhone while my
buddies and I smiled.

In our college apartment, dressed in our ugly Christmas sweaters,
Blake posed as the dad with his arm across Mike, the mom. Pat and I
held up gifts like happy kids at Christmas.

Click.

The fake family moment was fleeting. An hour later we were on the
field at practice.

During Christmas week at the University of Wisconsin, other students left campus for holiday family time while football players stayed.
Instead of eating a big meal with loved ones and opening up gifts, we
spent the week getting the stuffing kicked out of us on the field.

> *Someone told him, "Your mother and brothers are standing
> outside, wanting to speak to you." He replied to him, "Who
> is my mother, and who are my brothers?" Pointing to his dis-
> ciples, he said, "Here are my mother and my brothers. For
> whoever does the will of my Father in heaven is my brother
> and sister and mother" (Matthew 12:47-50).*

Jesus never meant that we should disown family or form new odd-
looking families like in the goofy picture with my teammates, but
rather that we should be closely related to those who do the will of
His Father in heaven. Through high school, college, and into the NFL,
away from home, players on one team become family, even dressing

up in ugly sweaters for a Christmas Instagram moment. We are in one place, doing the will of the coach—our dad—for the team.

Jesus's disciples left behind families to follow Christ and spread the Good News. While family relationships should be our closest ones, in dorms, battlegrounds, or workplaces we also find family; those working together toward one purpose. Christians also ought to be united on one team—brothers and sisters in Christ—working toward the goal that leads us to the final victory—heaven, our ultimate home.

Huddle

A large circle formation taken by the players on the field prior to the start of the play. In the huddle, the quarterback (offense) or linebacker (defense) informs the players which play will be run, along with words of encouragement.

I can't go," Phil Supernaw said. "I'll just be a burden."

"Huddle!" I said to my teammates. Phil, a tight end for the Texans, had suffered a football injury—a broken foot—and couldn't walk. My buddies and I wanted to get out of Houston and attend a concert in Austin, but we couldn't leave Phil behind.

"We'll find a wheelchair." Ben Jones grabbed his smart phone and started searching.

"No player should be left behind." Cody White pumped a fist in the air. "You're coming with us."

I clapped my hands and then pointed. "You two. Interlock arms and make a chair. Carry him. I'll get my pickup."

We hefted Phil out to my truck and drove around town in search of the medical supply store. Finally, with the wheelchair in back and my buddies in the truck, I parked at the concert. We lifted Phil into the chair and wheeled him to Will Call, where our tickets were being held.

A smiling young woman behind the counter glanced at the tickets. Her smile faded and she shook her head. "These are for the general public. There's no wheelchair access."

"If one of us can't get in, none of us will go." I crossed my arms. The others nodded.

Let us consider how we may spur one another on toward love and good deeds, not giving up meeting together, as some are in the habit of doing, but encouraging one another—and all the more as you see the Day approaching (Hebrews 10:24-25).

The girl looked at Phil and sighed. "Y'all are so sweet to care for your friend." She smiled. "Wait here. I'll be right back."

A few minutes later she returned with special tickets to the VIP area close to the stage and backstage passes too!

Huddles are used in sports to bring everyone together, discuss strategies, and encourage individuals. On offense, the quarterback relays the plays in the huddle. On defense, the captain relays the coach's instructions for the proper alignment and how to defend the expected play. Words of encouragement are passed in the huddle to keep each other motivated and to keep the game plan in sight.

In our huddle, we had decided we couldn't attend a concert and leave a teammate behind, especially one who was injured and downhearted. In the end, our commitment toward each other gained us VIP passes and we all had a great time, a night we'll never forget.

Vince Lombardi once said, "Individual commitment to a group effort—that is what makes a team work, a company work, a society work, a civilization work."

Got a player on your team who is weak? Downhearted? Are you? Gather your team, discuss strategy, and encourage one another. If the plan benefits the entire team, a successful outcome will follow.

Illegal Contact

A penalty resulting from a defensive player interfering
with an offensive receiving player more than five
yards from the line of scrimmage, allowing the
receivers to run unimpeded after five yards and not
get mauled. The result of the penalty is five yards
and an automatic first down in favor of the offense.

In my freshman year with the Wisconsin Badgers, my vision blurred during practice. Unable to wear my new diabetic pump during practice, I'd been sluggish and unable to concentrate. I knew the signs. High blood sugar.

The tight end coach sighed. "Diabetes issues?"

I nodded.

"Sit out until you have it under control."

Diabetes was making illegal contact with my football career, taking me out of the game. Seated on the bench, Mike Moll, the trainer, checked my blood sugar.

He affirmed what I already knew. I grabbed my pump and gave myself the correct dose of insulin.

I rested my head in my hands. "I'm doing my best to keep regulated, but it's been like this all week. I can't concentrate or even stay on the field for long periods of time. The coaches are getting frustrated with me. I'm getting frustrated with myself."

"Can't you wear your pump?" Mike asked.

"I wish, but it'll get banged up on the field."

"Maybe we can figure out a way to make this work. Follow me."

In the locker room, Mike traced my insulin pump on the back plate of my shoulder pads and then cut out a compartment for my pump. We used leg wrap to secure it from falling out of the hole he cut, and then he stuck it inside my pads.

When I got into the NFL, I showed the trainer what I was using and they sent the design to Douglas, the maker of our shoulder pads. They custom-made a special back plate that protects my pump, and that's what I use on the field to keep me regulated.

> *I turned my mind to understand, to investigate and to search out wisdom and the scheme of things and to understand the stupidity of wickedness and the madness of folly (Ecclesiastes 7:25).*

In life, problems rail against you. It's not fair, but you have to deal with your circumstances and make the best of them. Sometimes you'll get bumped and banged around, but how you react to getting kicked in the gut defines you as a person. Diabetes is like an illegal contact, a kick in the gut, a punch in the mouth. It's like a defensive player interfering with me, an offensive receiving player. I have to deal with the disease, fair or not.

Wearing my insulin pump keeps me regulated while on the field. I live like a person hooked up to an IV; my pump needs to be attached to me at all times.

There weren't any reference points to search for an answer to my problem with wearing my pump, so my trainer found a solution. If you can't handle the obstacles and interferences that block you from your goals, figure out a solution or ask for help from others. God will give us wisdom to handle life's blows and interferences if we ask Him for it.

Injured Reserve

A list of players on each team who are off the 53-man roster and involved in treatment and recovery for injuries.

oward the end of my junior year at Wisconsin, I was really beat up, to say the least. The week before the championship game with Michigan State, I'd struggled to make it through practice. I hid the pain. I couldn't tell anyone I was hurt. The Badgers had a great shot at getting into the Rose Bowl and the team needed me.

The day of the big game arrived. Getting into my stance was incredibly painful. My back ached. I had a bruised AC joint in my shoulder. Reminding myself not all players are perfectly healthy in football but still play through pain, I sucked it up. There's a huge difference between being hurt and being injured. Going into that game with a high ankle sprain, I was only hurt. I gritted my teeth, took some ibuprofen, said a prayer, and played on.

> Be sober-minded; be watchful. Your adversary the devil prowls around like a roaring lion, seeking someone to devour. Resist him, firm in your faith, knowing that the same kinds of suffering are being experienced by your brotherhood throughout the world. And after you have suffered a little while, the God of all grace, who has called you to his eternal glory in Christ, will himself restore, confirm, strengthen, and establish you (1 Peter 5:8-10 ESV).

Humans aren't meant to play football. Each year, the guys drafted into the NFL are bigger, stronger, and faster. A lineman used to weigh 180 pounds. Now some receivers are more than 230 pounds and hitting a lot harder. Football is full of testosterone-driven meatheads, and the clashing of these large, athletic, ego-driven humans causes players to be put on injured reserve or taken out of the game for life.

I played through the pain against Michigan State that day, as did most of my teammates. We won, became division champions, and went on to play in the Rose Bowl against Oregon on New Year's Day.

Just as football isn't pain-free, neither is life. It only gets tougher and tougher. The Bible mentions suffering quite frequently, and there's no getting away from it as long as we live.

Players can be stuck on the injured reserve list for the season or even cut from the team due to injuries. The NFL may abandon us, but God never abandons His children, no matter how our injuries—physical or emotional—have left us feeling sidelined from the game of life.

God promises to help us through our troubles, and He will restore, confirm, strengthen, and establish us. You can't take His grace in the form of a pill, but it's there. Whatever pain you are going through, you're never alone. Pray, and God will get you through.

Jersey Numbers

Jersey numbers are assigned by particular positions.
Lower numbers are for quarterbacks and other skilled
players. Numbers between 50 and 79 are for linemen.
This is done intentionally so the officials can distinguish
who is who during a play. Linemen are not eligible
to receive a pass or run downfield during a pass, so
the numbers allow for easy spotting for penalties.

When the Chargers signed me to their practice squad, I was offered a few available jersey numbers. I'd been number 82 in college and also for the Saints, and number 89 for the Houston Texans. My brother, Nick, five years younger than me, had been choosing my jersey number since third grade youth center football.

Nick received a scholarship to play football for the Ragin' Cajuns when I was number 82 with the New Orleans Saints. That number was not available, so he chose the closest number to mine, 81.

In San Diego I wanted a fresh start, a new number. I thought about Nick and how he always looked up to me, followed in my footsteps, and often took a back seat to me. This time, I decided to choose number 81—his number—to honor him.

Do nothing out of selfish ambition or vain conceit. Rather, in humility value others above yourselves, not looking to your own interests but each of you to the interests of the others. In your relationships with one another, have the same mindset as Christ Jesus: Who, being in very nature God, did not consider equality with God something to be used to his own advantage; rather, he made himself nothing by taking the very nature of a servant, being made in human likeness. And being found in appearance as a man, he humbled

himself by becoming obedient to death—even death on a
cross! (Philippians 2:3-8).

In football, numbers identify the position played and the battle is on to be the best in that position. True to their importance on the field, quarterbacks are given the first numbers. In life we aren't assigned a number and have to make our way, often battling to earn a top place in school, job, or whatever we do. But pushing forward to become number one doesn't mean putting others down or climbing over them to get ahead. Being number one isn't about looking out for number one. That tends to backfire, and it's not the way God tells us to be. If the Son of God can lower Himself to come down from heaven and become a servant to men, even taking our sins upon Himself and dying a horrific death, shouldn't we consider Him and others before ourselves? My little brother is one of the most humble, Christlike people I know. He always puts others first. Is there someone in your life who looks up to you, a friend who always takes a back seat to others? What can you do to honor that person?

Kickoff

A free kick (the receiving team can't make an
attempt to block it) that puts the ball into play. A
kickoff is used at the start of the first and third
quarters and after every touchdown or field goal.

When I was a baby, just a week old, I was hospitalized and about to have a blood transfusion. I'd turned yellow with jaundice and my bilirubin count was soaring. The story my mom tells is that while two nurses turned away from my incubator to prepare an IV for my head, a loud crash sounded. Everyone turned in surprise to discover I'd kicked open the incubator door.

> *You are a chosen people, a royal priesthood, a holy nation,*
> *God's special possession, that you may declare the praises of*
> *him who called you out of darkness into his wonderful light.*
> *Once you were not a people, but now you are the people of*
> *God; once you had not received mercy, but now you have*
> *received mercy (1 Peter 2:9-10).*

At kickoff, the ball is kicked as far downfield as possible. It's an exciting moment. No matter what happened during the last game or quarter, a kickoff fills the crowd and players with a thrilling rush of enthusiasm. It's a new start, a chance to be redeemed from a recent loss or a boost of enthusiasm to score points. But like life, the game is challenging and the defense will try to stop you.

To this day I'm not sure if my baby kick was in protest against everything coming at me, but it sure did shock everyone in the room. The nurses checked my levels again, and it turned out I didn't need the IV. My bilirubin counts had lowered and I was good to go! I got a fresh start in my new young life.

God chose the Savior of the world to come to us as an infant, but unlike us, He was born sinless. Through Jesus we have an opportunity to start fresh, come out of dark shadows, and embrace the Living Light. Like the start of a new game at kickoff, Jesus offers forgiveness and salvation. The score is zero and the gridiron is open. A new opportunity waits to kick the ball and start the action rolling toward your goal.

What keeps you from moving forward? What prevents you from being the person God intends you to be? What door do you need to kick down to move into the light of Christ?

Loose Ball

A ball that is lying or rolling on the field after a
fumble, not in possession of either team.

We had just moved from Pennsylvania to Michigan a couple days before school started—me in the third grade, my sister in second. On the first day of school, my mom dropped us off and gave us instructions to ride the bus home. She'd repeated the bus number over and over to me that morning so I wouldn't forget it, and she even stuck a note in my pocket and taped one inside my backpack along with our new address.

We got on the right bus after school. One by one, kids got off. Down to just Betsy and me, the driver stopped in the middle of nowhere and opened the door. "This is your stop."

"But it doesn't look familiar," I said. "I don't think this is it. I don't see my house anywhere."

He flipped down the visor. "This is your stop. See you tomorrow."

I grabbed my sister's hand and we stepped off the bus and stood at the edge of a wheat field. The road sign at the corner read "Eighteen Mile Road."

"We're lost!" Tears welled up in Betsy's eyes.

"This is Eighteen Mile Road. We live on Eighteen Mile Road. Worst case scenario, we have to walk eighteen miles to find our house."

"Wahhhhhh!"

That didn't help. "Our house is just up there. I'm sure of it."

She sniffed. "Really?"

"Yep. Let's go." I had no idea where our house was, but I was glad she stopped crying.

We walked for a little while on that empty road with not a car or house in sight, just trees and fields. I was scared, but I kept telling my sister the house was just ahead. Truth was, we were two lost kids, loose on the field and not in possession of anyone. I feared we might never be found.

> *But while he was still a long way off, his father saw him and was filled with compassion for him; he ran to his son, threw his arms around him and kissed him. The son said to him, "Father, I have sinned against heaven and against you. I am no longer worthy to be called your son." But the father said to his servants, "Quick! Bring the best robe and put it on him. Put a ring on his finger and sandals on his feet. Bring the fattened calf and kill it. Let's have a feast and celebrate. For this son of mine was dead and is alive again; he was lost and is found." So they began to celebrate (Luke 15:20-24).*

"Jake! Betsy!" Far down the road, my mom appeared like a mirage. She and my little brother ran toward us. When she reached us, my mom knelt and gathered both of us into her arms.

Later, my mom called the school and ripped the principal a new one, explaining that anything could have happened to us on that lonely road. She'd been waiting at the end of the driveway, watching for us, and she had no idea why the bus hadn't brought us home.

Having been lost, we really celebrated our reuniting. The prodigal son in Luke must have felt like us in that moment, lost, away from his family, and not belonging anywhere until his father reclaimed him as his own.

We are like that with God when away from Him and lost—lost in our sin and rebellion like a loose ball rolling on the field, poised to be claimed by either side. God is like the offensive player on the field, scrambling to take possession of us, like our mom finally did that day. Along the way in life, it's easy to get lost. Coming home is sometimes more about God finding us. Whatever situation you get yourself in, however far you get from God, trust that He's out there looking for you. Keep moving on with your eyes focused ahead.

Mike Backer

The QB of the defense. The Mike Backer is in
charge of getting the entire defense set and
the play called. The Mike Backer is normally
the biggest and hardest hitting linebacker.

Big Lee Ziemba stared me down from the T-ball mound. Lee, a future
blue-chip offensive tackle, was one of the biggest humans I'd met in
Arkansas. By the fifth grade, he stood more than six feet tall and threw
the meanest fastball in Little League. Stepping up to bat, I swallowed
the lump in my throat. Lee wound up and unfurled the ball. Terror
gripped me. The ball crushed me in the ribs and laid me out, gasping
for breath. For a second I thought I was moving toward the light.

After that game, I stood at the edge of the batter's box and flinched
every time the ball was pitched to me. I finished out the last few games
and never stepped onto a baseball field again.

> *God is our refuge and strength, an ever-present help in trou-
> ble. Therefore we will not fear, though the earth give way
> and the mountains fall into the heart of the sea, though its
> waters roar and foam, and the mountains quake with their
> surging (Psalm 46:1-3).*

Today, Lee Ziemba is an NFL offensive lineman. Back in the fifth
grade, he was a monster who threw a mighty pitch that ended my baseball career. The Ziemba fear factor changed me from a first baseman
hitting home runs to a washed-up benchwarmer, cowering in the dug-
out while my mom fussed at the coach to put me in the game.

I wasn't afraid of Lee; he was my friend. We later became high
school football teammates. Since, I've played against many Lee Ziemba
types. We call them Mike Backers—big, hard-hitting linebackers. They

can scare the life out of you. You have to face your fears and will yourself to take on those monsters on the football field.

Fear is useless. It makes you question yourself, your life, and your faith. Few things are more destructive.

Are you struggling with fear? Are you scared to take the next step in a job or a relationship? Are you afraid to make an important decision? Do the Mike Backers in your life seem too big to handle?

These are times to find strength in God's Word. The Bible assures us that even if the earth gives way and the mountains fall into the heart of the sea, we should not fear. God can give us courage and deliver us from fear before it grows as big as a crushingly powerful Mike Backer.

National Signing Day

Normally the first Wednesday in February, National
Signing Day is set aside for high school seniors
to sign a National Letter of Intent with a college
that is a member of the United States National
Collegiate Athletic Association (NCAA).

Results on the field proved I was a decent high school football player, but would college recruiters know my worth?

I wanted to play football for the University of Wisconsin Badgers because their offense was a perfect fit for a tight end like me. My parents grew up in Wisconsin, and my grandparents' house wasn't far from the campus. I sent film to the recruiting coaches. Disappointingly, they never got back to me. The Badgers didn't recruit in Arkansas, so I wasn't even on their radar as a top high school prospect.

I visited the college in spite of their seeming lack of interest. UW fit the mold of my image of the perfect school—it was located in a big college town and had tradition, excellent academic and athletic programs, and a good reputation. I was sold, but I couldn't go unless I was offered a football scholarship.

After leaving the campus with my dad, I stared out at the Wisconsin farmland. "I wish they'd give me a chance and watch me play. I'm sure they'd give me a scholarship."

"They don't know your worth," my dad said.

A few weeks later, I got a scholarship offer from the University of Arkansas, followed by an offer from Kansas State, Mississippi State, Missouri State, Tulsa, Georgia Tech, and a few other colleges. It was like Christmas, and I was over-the-top excited. I was valuable to nearly ten big colleges in the South. Amazing!

Though I'd done nothing to change the recruiting coaches' minds, Wisconsin took note of me. They said they would like to come down to Arkansas and watch me play. Instead, I said I'd come to them, participate in an upcoming camp.

At camp, they timed me in the 40-yard dash and shuttle and had me bench-press and compete against other top prospects they had recruited. After the day was over, head coach Bret Bielema brought me into his office and offered me a scholarship. On National Signing Day, I signed with the Badgers.

> Are not two sparrows sold for a penny? Yet not one of them will fall to the ground outside your Father's care. And even the very hairs of your head are all numbered. So don't be afraid; you are worth more than many sparrows (Matthew 10:29-31).

There's a ballad—"The Touch of the Master's Hand" by Myra Welch—regarding a battered and scarred violin being auctioned off. The auctioneer, seeing its condition, doesn't think it's worth anything. He starts the bids at $1. But then the unexpected happens. An old man steps forward, takes the violin, and begins to play. The story tells of a "melody pure and sweet as a caroling angel sings" emanating from the old violin. The auctioneer restarts the bids at $1,000. The ballad ends with:

> But the Master comes, and the foolish crowd
> Never can quite understand
> The worth of a soul and the change that is wrought
> By the touch of the Master's hand.

Sometimes we get frustrated, beat down, and discouraged because we know our worth but others don't. Sometimes we doubt if even God deems us worthy. Our worth isn't established by our experiences. It's not measured by what others think or even what we think of ourselves. Our worth is established by the Master and is completely dependent upon what God thinks of us and how He can transform us.

Whoever is looking you over, determining your worth in any situation—scholarship, job, relationship—ultimately your true worth depends on the touch of the Master's hand as you turn your life over to Him. Signing your life over to God is the best decision you can make.

Nicknames

A name given to a player or a team that best describes that person or team's attributes.

The nickname "Monsters of the Midway" belonged to one of the best defenses ever, the 1985 Chicago Bears. Pittsburgh's "Steel Curtain" and Dallas's "Doomsday Defense" were nicknames given to those teams for obvious reasons. The Vikings are called "Purple People Eaters."

People are given nicknames too. J.J. Watt—my teammate on the Badgers and then in the NFL on the Texans—is called J.J. "Swat" because of his ability to deflect passes. Jerry Rice was called "The G.O.A.T" (Greatest Of All Time).

> *God exalted him to the highest place and gave him the name that is above every name, that at the name of Jesus every knee should bow, in heaven and on earth and under the earth, and every tongue acknowledge that Jesus Christ is Lord, to the glory of God the Father (Philippians 2:9-11).*

Taking a break after summer classes at the University of Wisconsin, four of my buddies and I went bowling. We decided we all needed a nickname. Sam Spitz, a fullback who loved to run and hit anything that moved on the football field, was given the name "Hebrew Hammer." We called Jake Current "Country Bear" because he was a burly country boy. They called me "Sugar-Free JB" because of my diabetes and the diet I had to keep to.

We earn nicknames because of who we are. God gave Jesus His name and told the angel Gabriel to announce it to Mary. It means "God saves." While Jerry Rice may have been the greatest receiver of all time, God is the greatest of all.

Off Season

The period of time between the Super Bowl and
the beginning of the next football season.

On California's Bear Mountain, my friends and I decided to have
some fun and dress out of the ordinary one day while we went
snowboarding. I was an American cowboy in jean shorts, wearing an
American flag sleeveless shirt, and a red-white-and-blue bandana. I figured if I wrecked, someone would save the guy dressed in the American
flag first. Chris Marsh had the same idea and wore short shorts and red-
white-and-blue suspenders. Max Craddock, a friend from Los Ange-
les, was rocking a majestic lion suit on the slopes and singing songs
from *The Lion King*.

Our flashy costumes and endless laughter gained us a lot of friends
that day. Parents with kids approached us with cameras and asked
for photos. Men handed out business cards, offering free places to
stay. One guy gave me his daughter's phone number. Our contagious
joy and happy personalities even earned us kisses on the cheeks from
elderly ladies.

> *I commend the enjoyment of life, because there is nothing*
> *better for a person under the sun than to eat and drink and*
> *be glad. Then joy will accompany them in their toil all the*
> *days of the life God has given them under the sun (Ecclesi-*
> *astes 8:15).*

In the NFL, the regular season is more mental than physical. The
game plan changes every week, so we have to adjust the plays for different defense. Every week is a different learning process. Off season is
a break from the mental process, but athletes must work hard at getting their bodies in prime shape for the upcoming season. Breaks now

and then, especially ones that involve physical activity, are well earned and appreciated. On the slopes, my buddies and I—serious football players, not serious snowboarders—wanted to have a good time, make friends, and be the party.

While working hard toward your goals, take time to cut loose and have fun. King Solomon, who probably wrote the book of Ecclesiastes, was known as the wisest king. If he's on board with having a good time, we ought to take his advice.

Offsetting Penalties

Offsetting penalties occur when a player on both sides of the ball—offense and defense—each has a penalty. As a result, the down is repeated and the distance remains the same.

At 17, with Kenny Chesney's "Summertime" blaring as we rode around in my Jeep, my friends and I thought we were too cool.

"Hey, I have cigars," one friend said. "Do you mind if we light up?"

"Go ahead." I couldn't smoke and drive a stick shift, but I didn't have a problem with my friends smoking...until I got home. The Jeep stunk. I grabbed a can of deodorizer from a shelf in the garage and blasted the vehicle. In the house I ran smack into my dad, empty can in hand. He raised an eyebrow.

I tossed the can in the trash. "Left gym clothes in my Jeep. Reeks."

I returned to grab my clothes, sniffed, and detected a faint odor. I pulled open the ash tray and found the source—cigar butts. I wrapped them in a paper towel and returned to the house hoping to bury them in the trash can. Again, my dad eyed me.

"Cookies from my friend's mom." I shoved the paper towel in a shoe box in my bedroom closet, making a mental note to take them out with the trash after my dad left for work the next day.

But I forgot about it, and a few days later, my dad discovered the tobacco. He mistook it for a joint and accused me of smoking weed. He freaked out and tore my room apart, looking for further evidence of drug use.

The Lord detests lying lips, but he delights in people who are trustworthy (Proverbs 12:22).

In football, offsetting penalties cancel out each other. The official, like God, is always watching. If you respond to an illegal play done to you, it will be seen. Offsetting penalties help no one. They only draw attention to yourself in a negative way. I did that with my dad, drawing unneeded and unwanted attention to myself because of my actions. Though my dad was wrong in his suspicions of me, I was just as wrong in my behavior that brought on those suspicions.

Lying is a violation against the rules of life, against God's rules. There are a ton of Bible verses about lying. Bottom line: God doesn't like it and neither do parents. I'd been warned, time and again: "If you're in trouble, tell the truth and the punishment will be less." That day, I hadn't done anything wrong—I hadn't even taken a puff off a cigar—and I probably would have just gotten away with a small lecture if I'd been honest. But I lied to avoid a hassle. Then I lied again. Proverbs 12:22 is right. Honesty, even in a dicey situation, will prove your trustworthiness.

Out of Position

Being out of position can occur in many ways,
but it happens when a player is in the wrong
spot for the play. It's most common on defense
or special teams when the player is in the wrong
gap or playing the wrong area of the field.

In the beginning of my first year of high school football, I was a wide receiver and one of the team's youngest players. I was doing great, getting reps and preparing for the first game. Then three days before the first game, the coach called me into the office.

"I need you to play offensive line. Matthew Huffmaster tore his ACL."

When you're a wide receiver, in the glory spot of catching the ball and making the big plays, the last thing you want is to get stuck on the offensive line. Blocking is the most inglorious job on the field.

The coach could probably tell from my sigh that I wasn't pleased. I was 16, 6 feet 5 and 240 pounds, playing varsity, and had the year mapped out as the guy whose name was going to be in the newspaper each week.

"I don't have anyone except you, Jake, who is physically and mentally ready to take the tackle position," Coach said.

To sweeten the deal, he promised to also play me as a defensive end.

I agreed, realizing that the game wasn't about me but about the team, and I wanted to win games more than anything. So I went out there each week, lining up next to my teammate, guard Smitty. Out of my normal position, he told me where to go and who to block until I had time to learn the new position.

Whoever exalts himself will be humbled, and whoever humbles himself will be exalted (Matthew 23:12 ESV).

I learned a really good lesson that freshman year, going from being a big shot and making all of the plays to a humble position. After that first season, Coach put me in as tight end.

Looking back, agreeing to take a spot on the team out of my position worked out great. The University of Wisconsin didn't offer an automatic scholarship. I had to go to camp and try out for a team whose tight ends did a lot of blocking. I was in a position to show I could play offensive line, block, and do the things I could never have done as a wide receiver. Playing offensive tackle that year gave me a good resume and a well-rounded skill set.

Don't be discouraged if for a season you have to do something you consider beneath you or that puts you out of position from your normal routine. You never know. You may be gaining a skill set that God will use in the bigger scheme of the plan He has for your life.

Penalty

A foul signified by the throwing of a yellow flag on
the field. A penalty can occur for many reasons
and the assessment of negative yards can vary from
five yards to the spot where the foul occurred.

In college, off-season workouts in the fall began at five in the morning. That didn't mean get up at five o'clock or be there at that time. It meant fully dressed, stretched, and conditioned when the clock hit five.

One morning close to five o'clock, one guy was missing from practice. We called him but he didn't answer. The coach wouldn't start practice until he got there, so we waited. Finally, with the coach's approval, we sent someone to get him from home. When he finally arrived, it was close to seven o'clock. Our coach rolled a comfy, cushioned leather desk chair to the middle of the field and told him to sit. Then he gave him a 36-ounce cup of Powerade and told him to sip it and watch the rest of us do the workout—twice! Once for us and once for him.

> *He did not enter by means of the blood of goats and calves;*
> *but he entered the Most Holy Place once for all by his own*
> *blood, thus obtaining eternal redemption (Hebrews 9:12).*

When one guy makes a mistake on the field—causes a penalty—the entire team pays the consequences, which often affects the outcome of the game.

We mess up for different reasons, sometimes from carelessness or temptation. Our teammate had stayed up late studying and fell asleep without setting his alarm. He certainly didn't do that on purpose, but we all paid the penalty. From that experience we put together a buddy system where everyone was responsible for one other person. Our teammate wasn't late again and neither was anyone else for the rest of the workouts during that off-season.

Jesus covers all of us. In the old days, before He was born, the priests shed the blood of goats and calves and other creatures to cover sins. Animals paid the price. That's one reason why Jesus is called the Lamb of God, the Sacrificial Lamb whose shed blood covers the sins of the world. Unlike the entire team that pays the price, Jesus, one man and the Son of God, paid the price for all humanity.

Guilt was all over our teammate's face as he sat in the center of the field and sipped Powerade while we worked out. When we sin against God—whether intentionally or not—we should think of ourselves like that guy who watched others pay the price for his mistake. That experience taught me two lessons: 1) to look out for a brother and 2) to be careful not to make mistakes that cause everyone else to suffer. Jesus's suffering took away our sin. That should make us think before sinning against His laws.

Personal Foul

An act of unsportsmanlike contact,
most common when players commit an act of
unnecessary roughness on the field.

On an extremely hot day during a seven-on-seven tournament, I was watching my younger brother, Nick, play in Tuscaloosa, Alabama. I made my way to a chair under an awning to escape the heat, always a factor with diabetes. An elderly lady approached and I offered my seat. A few minutes later, a middle-aged, heavy-set woman displaced the older woman saying, "I have to sit down. I have diabetes."

"I have diabetes too," I said. "You'll be all right. Don't take her seat."

The elderly lady, standing over her stolen seat, looked at me. "You're too fit to have diabetes."

While the diabetic woman sipped her sugary soda and spilled Twinkies all over herself, a friendly conversation began between the two ladies and myself about the difference between type 1 and type 2 diabetes.

God gave us a spirit not of fear but of power and love and self-control (2 Timothy 1:7 ESV).

Not taking care of our health is like a personal foul against ourselves. In football, personal fouls are usually avoidable: unnecessary roughness, grabbing a face mask, an illegal block on the knees of a vulnerable player, or a blow to the head of the quarterback.

Unlike the middle-aged woman with type 2 diabetes experiencing difficulties due to a disease she has control over, type 1 diabetes is different. I didn't get diabetes from eating too much sugar. Type 1 diabetes is an autoimmune disease completely different from type 2. Type 2 is curable. Type 1 is not. Many type 2 diabetics could rid themselves of the disease if they would work out and eat healthy.

Anger built inside me as the elderly woman fanned herself in the sun while the younger woman sipped her soda in the shade and complained about diabetes. The hot sun also affects the elderly. Finally, the seated woman got up and offered my seat back to the poor, overheated grandma.

I don't judge people with type 2 diabetes because I understand there are factors specific to each person with the disease, but those who complain about suffering from abuse they have done to their own bodies ought to take steps to help themselves.

Unhealthy lifestyles—bad eating habits, no exercise—make way for disease and illness to step in and take down an otherwise healthy body. It's hard to feel sorry for someone who is not taking care of their body.

If changing our lifestyle seems too difficult in any area, we can ask God for help and for the wisdom and strength to do what we can to change. As Scripture says, God gives us the power of self-control.

Play Clock

The timer that counts down the amount of time the
offensive team has to begin the play by snapping the
ball. After a play is finished and the ball has been placed
in its new location, the referee will start the play clock. In
the NFL, the offense has forty seconds to snap the ball.

After the Texans cut me from their regular roster, I went to the Chiefs on practice squad. During my first day I met a player who had also just arrived in Kansas City. He'd played on a Canadian arena football team for three years and was thrilled to finally get a shot in the NFL, his ultimate goal. We signed our contracts the same day. With tears in his eyes, he spoke about how hard he worked. His wife and kids were excited to be moving to Kansas City.

The next day I discovered he was gone. Cut the same day he was given a contract. The Chiefs replaced him with a new receiver. There are no guarantees in the NFL. When another player is deemed as someone who can serve the team better, you're gone without a second thought. Career ended.

Teach us to number our days, that we may gain a heart of wisdom (Psalm 90:12).

I prayed my teammate would get another shot with a different team. That's a tough situation for a guy with a family.

Jobs end. Relationships end. We work hard to achieve a goal, think we've made it, and then everything changes. Life is like that sometimes. Successes are often short lived. Like the time clock that ticks off until the end of the game, there's a bigger time clock ticking down the days of our life or the time in one place or situation.

Only God can see our life's play clock. He knows the perfect timing for everything. The best we can do is pray we gain a heart of wisdom so that we can serve Him all the days of our lives.

Play-Off Games

Games played in the post-season to determine the
champion. After the regular season has concluded, the
teams with the best record move on to the play-offs.

Never take anything for granted." Mike McCoy's eyes scanned the
meeting room. When the head coach of the San Diego Chargers
spoke the night before a play-off game, we listened.

"There are guys in this room who have played for more than ten
years, waiting their entire career for an opportunity like this."

Though Coach was talking to everyone, as a second-year player
about to experience my first play-off game, I was definitely an intended
receiver of his words. *Never take anything for granted.*

Why, you do not even know what will happen tomorrow.
What is your life? You are a mist that appears for a little
while and then vanishes (James 4:14).

Humbled to be a part of the San Diego Chargers team on the eve of
a play-off game, I thanked God for the opportunity and vowed to give
my best. The next day, the game was like nothing I'd ever experienced
before. The stakes were high. Everything happened fast. The moment,
fleeting. But what a memorable game! A highlight of my life!

Mike McCoy's words often return to me. Life is a gift. Each day, a
new game to be played. We should never take anything for granted. We
never know what will happen tomorrow. Having a grateful heart for
each day is the only way to live.

Position

Eleven players from each team are on the field at a time, and each player has a position, role, and responsibility to complete the offense, defense, or special teams.

I am a firstborn. My little brother, Nick, five years younger than me, was the last addition to the gang. In his baby years, he was happiest in one position—cradled in my lap, watching the screen as I played video games. At first it was a pain, but I got used to playing with him. My favorite games were Madden sports games. It wasn't long before Nick's position changed. He soon sat beside me, holding his own controller. Later, he was a real competitor, learning the football positions and eventually becoming a formidable challenger.

At age 17 I zipped up my suitcase, ready to leave for college.

"Let's play one more game before you go." Nick wiped a tear on his sleeve.

I took my position on the floor with Nick beside me. He beat me. I didn't even let him. Soon the game ended. The hardest thing about leaving for college was watching my little brother tear up when I said my final goodbye.

While I was in college, I got a call from Nick. "Hey, I'm with my friends, playing you on Madden NCAA 2012."

By that time I was actually in the college football video game, and he was proud to be picking me as a player. "Give me extra strength," I said. "Pump up my muscles."

"Right now I'm giving you a really huge backside and little chicken legs."

Chuckles came through the phone.

Be kindly affectionate to one another with brotherly love, in honor giving preference to one another (Romans 12:10 NKJV).

Through the laughter I could hear Nick's pride and love. When he was a kid, he would sometimes drive me nuts with always wanting to hang out with me and my friends, but I had done my best to bring him into my world. It's what a big brother should do. Most of my friends were cool with Nick hanging out with us.

Now when we get together, I want to spend all my free time hanging out with Nick and his friends. He's also a football player, a tight end. Same position I play.

There's nothing like having a brother, especially one like Nick. God says to give preference to one another. That means putting that person first, be it a brother or one who is like a brother to you. The paybacks are great.

Possession

A term to describe who has the ball. The offensive
team has possession of the ball. A turnover
can cause a team to lose possession.

Coach Rudolph, my tight end coach for the Wisconsin Badgers, once said, "Life is tough. So is football. Don't ever let someone set your limitations."

Having diabetes, those words rang true for me. My diagnosis shocked me. A few naysayers recommended giving up my dreams. If I'd accepted diabetes as a limitation, I would have lost possession of my goals. If I had felt sorry for myself and used diabetes as an excuse to be lazy and soft, my football career would have ended.

Be watchful, stand firm in the faith, act like men, be strong
(1 Corinthians 16:13 ESV).

Though a team loses possession of the ball for part of the game, they can't lose sight of the ultimate goal: Winning. Losing possession of our faith can happen when we lose sight of God, when we don't feel Him working in our lives, or when others cast doubt about us or our faith. We want to give up. But God is always there. Without holding firmly to Him, we can't get anywhere in life.

Have other goals, even good ones, blocked your eyes from Christ? Are you trusting in His Word and taking all your worries and cares to Him in prayer, acknowledging that He has them in His hands? Don't lose possession of your goals. Though life is hard, don't ever let anyone or anything set your limitations.

Practice

The amount of time spent getting ready for the next season or game. It includes time in the weight room, running on the track, hours of watching film, and, of course, actually hitting each other on the field.

The way you practice is the way you'll play." My tight end coach preached those words nearly every day during practice at the University of Wisconsin.

Intensity during practice has to be just as intense as the game itself, or success will not be in your favor. What happens in the game is the result of what's been happening all week.

By the time the play clock starts and I'm in my stance on the line of scrimmage, what we practiced becomes muscle memory. My ears are turned off to the roar of the crowd and the defensive play calls. The only voice I hear is that of my quarterback as he calls out the signals.

At the "blue 80" my body knows what to do. Release, step, and extend my arms to press the defender off the line of scrimmage as I rotate my body into the hole to shield my running back—that all becomes second nature. Practice makes perfect.

> *Be perfect, therefore, as your heavenly Father is perfect (Matthew 5:48).*

Daily practice is tough, but repetition fine-tunes our body and trains it to instinctively react when necessary. The same goes for our spiritual life. Studying God's Word, going to church, and surrounding ourselves with faithful souls ground us in our faith. We become trained Christians, knowing right from wrong and how to react in any given situation. We become confident leaders. Are you practicing your faith enough so that you are a skilled Christian, instinctively able to react in the way Christ would in all situations?

Practice Film

*Every snap, every play you run in college is
filmed. Every little detail is captured so you can
be praised or ripped apart by coaches.*

You didn't stay on block long enough to spring the runner!" Coach
Rudolph yelled while we watched college practice film. "Every
extra effort, step, hand placement, and pad level will be the difference
between winning and losing."

Before the coach says anything, I'm already my hardest critic. I watch
everything on film and never want to let any teammate or coach down.

On the field, players are judged and penalties are given. After the
game, film is judgment time. You judge yourself, questioning if you
did everything right to help the team win.

> *If we were more discerning with regard to ourselves, we
> would not come under such judgment. Nevertheless, when
> we are judged in this way by the Lord, we are being disci-
> plined so that we will not be finally condemned with the
> world (1 Corinthians 11:31-32).*

In football, a coach's corrections help us improve so we don't make
the same mistakes. Corrections are also mercy, and it's best when they
are done during practice film review so that when thousands of fans
are watching an actual game, we don't make a mistake that costs the
team the win.

In all life situations, we should judge ourselves to ensure we are
doing everything right to help the body of Christ. Sometimes we get
judged by others, and that's not a bad thing. If someone else corrects
you, take it well. They might be saving you from making that same mistake again during a critical moment.

Pump Fake

A tactic used by a quarterback in which he fakes a throw by moving his arm and shoulders as if throwing but doesn't release the ball. Ideally, a pump fake can cause a defensive player to be out of position as they react, which can allow for the receiver to be open and connected with the quarterback on a successful throw.

I stood outside the nurse's office before the last class of the day.

"Blood sugar low?" The Rogers High School nurse looked me over.

I couldn't lie. I shook my head.

"Come in. Sit down."

Even though I sometimes faked low blood sugar to get out of class, the school nurse always had my number, literally. She only had to check my blood sugar and see my numbers to prove if I was faking, so I was straight with her. I sat down and she pulled up a chair across from me.

"Got a problem. I've been stressing over it all day. I found out this morning that our end of the year project is due today in my next class and I'm not prepared. I've also got a big game tonight."

The nurse stood. "Yes, you're low." She went to the sink and brought me a cup of water. "Better drink this orange juice." She winked at me and smiled.

For the rest of the next class period, I stayed in the office. The nurse sat with me and we talked about life, football, diabetes, and other worries on my mind.

I really appreciated her. She always took time to listen. She would sometimes share a funny story or just be a good friend, going above and beyond by handing me a cup of orange juice even when I wasn't faking low blood sugar to get out of class.

"I was hungry, and you gave Me something to eat; I was thirsty, and you gave Me something to drink; I was a stranger, and you invited Me in; naked, and you clothed Me; I was sick, and you visited Me; I was in prison, and you came to Me." Then the righteous will answer Him, saying, "Lord, when did we see You hungry, and feed You, or thirsty, and give You something to drink? And when did we see You a stranger, and invite You in, or naked, and clothe You? And when did we see You sick, or in prison, and come to You?" The King will answer and say to them, "Truly I say to you, to the extent that you did it to one of these brothers of Mine, even the least of them, you did it to Me" (Matthew 25:35-40 NASB).

Having diabetes challenges a person mentally as well as physically. Many nurses are great nurturers who know how to delve deeper, beyond the physical effects of the disease, into a person's mental health. That day my school nurse covered for me, even though it was my fault for not completing my project. Other days, when I really needed orange juice, she'd probe deeper, asking questions about life and how I was managing. She could read my emotions as well as a defender being faced by an excellent pump fake.

A pump fake is one thing, but when you are connecting with people off the football field, being honest with your feelings and efforts is of utmost importance. Never fake it and say everything is okay when it's not. Open up and talk to others you trust. It makes dealing with life so much easier when you can pour out what's on your heart. And like my high school nurse, if a friend appears troubled, dig a little deeper and reassure them. Whatever the issue, in the end it's all about how well we cared for others.

Quarterback

The quarterback is the leader on the field. He holds
a position on offense responsible for initiating the
majority of offensive plays. Quarterbacks must have
the capacity to analyze the defense and should
have a strong, accurate arm for downfield passes.

Before the beginning of a new NFL season, Scott Tolzien—quarter-back for the Green Bay Packers—and I finished an early morning run on a San Diego beach.

The sun rising over the top of the palm trees cast an orange hue over the water, signifying a brand-new day. When Scott and I had played for the Wisconsin Badgers a few years earlier, he had been my quarterback and I'd always looked to him for encouragement. Now we were on a bigger playing field and about to start a new season trying to secure a spot on our teams' roster.

We relaxed on the pier watching the sun rise over the water.

"What do you think it'll take to be successful in the NFL?" I asked.

Scott looked across the sea. "We have to walk into that huddle with total confidence. Not arrogance but without doubt that we are the best player in the huddle, that we will carry the team." He turned to me, and with fire in his words he said, "We're here because we are the best in our position, Jake. Don't forget that. Doubt kills more dreams than failure ever will."

> *Do not throw away your confidence; it will be richly rewarded. You need to persevere so that when you have done the will of God, you will receive what he has promised (Hebrews 10:35-36).*

The quarterback must have confidence on the field. He's the man in charge, the last person to allow the team to know he's scared. He's the leader, the one everyone is following. Confidence is a must under all circumstances.

The quarterback is also the central figure, the most prominent player on the field, kind of like how Moses was for the Israelites. On each play, he knows where each player should line up and what his job entails. The quarterback will assess where the defensive players will come from and where they will go, as he may need to call a change in the play, an audible.

On or off the field, Scott Tolzien is a great leader, and I always hold tight to his words. He encouraged me to have confidence that day, and so does Paul in his letter to the Hebrews. Doubt is a dream-killer. Don't be arrogant, but value confidence. It should never be thrown away. Count yourself as the best in your position and persevere. Confidence is a gift from God that we have to embrace so that in doing His will we receive what He has promised.

Red Zone

The area from the defending team's
twenty-yard line and the goal line, an area
considered within field goal range.

When I grew old enough to go pheasant hunting with my dad, Nick would cry when he was left behind. My dad would say, "It's a lot of work. Tall brush. Muddy swamps. Lots of walking."

One year we agreed he was old enough to tag along. He begged to carry a gun, so my dad let him carry his BB gun. We warned him it would be difficult, but Nick was so excited and insistent. He even woke us up at four o'clock to make sure he wasn't left behind.

My brother, always pushing to keep up to me, fought his way through tall grass. I felt sorry for him, and my dad and I carried him piggyback when we could. Finally, on our return and nearing the end of our day, tears welled up in his eyes. The brush was way over his head. He tripped and fell a few times, exhausted. Poor little guy. His body couldn't go on. I was twice his size and dead tired myself.

"There's a Snickers bar in the truck, little buddy," I said. "It's mine, but if you can beat me to the truck, it's yours." At the mention of the candy bar, Nick perked up. With new energy, he ran ahead and we let him beat us to the truck.

Blessed is the one who perseveres under trial because, having stood the test, that person will receive the crown of life that the Lord has promised to those who love him (James 1:12).

Entering the red zone, players are only 20 yards to the goal line. Having come so far, no matter how exhausted or hurt you are, a touchdown—the motivating factor—is only a short distance away. In the red zone, new energy fills each offensive player.

In the field, a promise of a candy bar became a motivating factor that gave my tired little brother enough energy to get to the truck.

We all need motivating factors; a reward at the end of a big task. The book of James promises the crown of life to those who love God. Following Christ is difficult, like getting to the end zone or walking through tall brush, fighting and pushing through when you're tired and ready to give up. But, more than a candy bar or a touchdown, the crown of life—salvation—promised by the Lord is the best reward. What's your motivating factor in life? Never give up. Keep pushing on toward your goals.

Return

When a player in possession of the ball
runs it back to his own end zone.

Coach Bielema handed me an email from ten-year-old Hunter Frederick. I was a freshman in college, and Hunter was the first child who reached out to me asking about diabetes. I connected with Hunter through email and then got him tickets for a spring game, spent time with him, and gave him a tour of the stadium. We met, hung out, and his family sent me care packages.

> *Give, and it will be given to you. A good measure, pressed down, shaken together and running over, will be poured into your lap. For with the measure you use, it will be measured to you (Luke 6:38).*

When Hunter reached out to me in college, I gave him just a little of my time, but the returns were great. Not only did I get great care packages from his family, I enjoyed spending time with him and experiencing the sense of fulfillment and peace in knowing I made a small difference in the life of another. Like a return in football, there is a sense of accomplishment when you return the ball into the end zone. There's also a sense of accomplishment when you give a little time to others. The words from Luke remind me of what my mother always said, "What goes around, comes around." Good advice from both.

Route

On every pass play, each player has a
designed route that ranges from distance and
direction to get open to catch a ball.

We'd just won the Big Ten championship and it was time to cele-brate. Leaving the stadium, a couple of frat guys patted me on the back and invited a few teammates and me to their house party.

Stepping into the house, we found the guy who had invited us holding a razor blade over a line of cocaine. He motioned us to join him.

My teammate jabbed me. "We don't belong here."

I nodded. "Let's go."

Later, we heard that party got busted and students were jailed. Many were expelled from school and never returned. Obviously, if we had stayed, we would have been in the wrong place at the wrong time and our playing days would have been over.

> *We are his workmanship, created in Christ Jesus for good works, which God prepared beforehand, that we should walk in them (Ephesians 2:10 ESV).*

A route is a particular path a player must follow. Routes must be run a particular depth and direction. If not, the play can result in an inter-ception or an incomplete.

Straying hurts everyone, whether it be our team or our family. When we veer off our route and step into places we don't belong, disas-ter is sure to trip us up.

God plans a specific route for us, a way in which we must follow, running forward to our goals. As a Christian, are you running the route God has called for you?

Running Back

A designated ball carrier. This is a player who
is handed the ball to gain rushing yards, who
normally always lines up in the backfield.

When I was a kid playing Madden 2005, I chose the Miami Dol-
phins because Ronnie Brown was the running back in the wildcat package the game featured. He jumped into the quarterback spot in
hopes of confusing the defense. At that position, Ronnie could run the
ball better than a quarterback could, so the wildcat package was born.
This was something the NFL had never experienced.

Years later, I had signed with the San Diego Chargers. To secure the
game, we needed to score and run time off the clock. Ronnie Brown
lined up behind me. A running play was called, and I made the block
that set Ronnie free for a touchdown. Assisting my childhood hero on
an NFL football field had me jumping up and down in the end zone,
waving my hands in the air and yelling with excitement. I couldn't
believe I got to help one of the game's greats make a play that led us to
victory and got us into the play-offs.

> *I have fought the good fight, I have finished the race, I have
> kept the faith. Now there is in store for me the crown of righ-
> teousness, which the Lord, the righteous Judge, will award
> to me on that day—and not only to me, but also to all who
> have longed for his appearing (2 Timothy 4:7-8).*

It took a long rookie year of getting cut several times to finally make
a roster, and there I was making big plays for the team, running along-
side the guy I selected as my best player in Madden 2005.

A running back is the hero when he takes the ball and runs downfield to a victory. Before Jesus ascended to heaven, He told the disciples
they would not be alone. He promised to be with them always. He sent

the Comforter, the Holy Spirit. Fire descended upon their heads and power to heal flowed through their fingers. After a long time of going from town to town with the Master, the disciples were handed the ball—given the power—by Jesus to heal and to transform in His name. And with the Holy Spirit, they pushed on toward victory after victory.

Running with Ronnie Brown toward victory was a great moment in my life, but accepting Christ and entering onto a field with the greats—Father, Son, and Holy Spirit—is an even better combination that gives me power to achieve the greatest victories in my life. You can experience that too.

Sack

When the quarterback is taken down behind the
line of scrimmage, resulting in a loss of yardage.

G o stand behind the field goal post. If I tell you to go in, I want you
to say, 'No Coach, I'll screw it up.' Now get out of my sight so I
don't have to look at you."

My heart sank to the pit of my gut. Like a quarterback getting
sacked, I experienced the ultimate humiliation and defeat. The coach,
frustrated with my performance, turned his back on me. I stepped into
the end zone, my head lowered in shame, hoping he wouldn't call me
to play and make me say the words, "No, Coach. I'll screw it up."

I'd graduated early from high school and was only 17, playing with
guys who were 23. I'd gone from being the king in high school, a super-
star physically stronger than everyone, to a broken, falling, shadow of
a star. I struggled with learning the plays and kept making mistakes.
On top of that, I battled diabetes. By the end of my first year, I was in
constant pain, tired of put-downs, and wanted to quit. No part of me
wanted to go on and play in the NFL.

I was sacked, done.

> *Who shall separate us from the love of Christ? Shall trouble
> or hardship or persecution or famine or nakedness or danger
> or sword? As it is written: "For your sake we face death all
> day long; we are considered as sheep to be slaughtered." No,
> in all these things we are more than conquerors through him
> who loved us. For I am convinced that neither death nor life,
> neither angels nor demons, neither the present nor the future,
> nor any powers, neither height nor depth, nor anything else
> in all creation, will be able to separate us from the love of
> God that is in Christ Jesus our Lord (Romans 8:35-39).*

Michael Jordan is quoted as saying, "I've missed more than nine thousand shots in my career. I've lost almost three hundred games. Twenty-six times, I've been trusted to take the game winning shot and missed. I've failed over and over and over again in my life. And that is why I succeed."

Knocked flat is never what we want to have happen in a sport or in life. Failure is one of the ugly realities everyone faces. You can't get away from it. But what matters most is how you handle it. From sports figures to Bible characters, the ones who really stand out are the ones who failed but refused to give up. If the apostle Paul, once a killer of Christians, quit at the first sign of trouble, we wouldn't have his letters to the Romans or many other books of the Bible. He met with a ton of troubles once he became a follower of Christ, but God's grace helped him to overcome any situation. The mature Christian is one who embraces failures as rungs on the ladder to success. Every sacked quarterback gets back up, huddles the team, and calls another play.

By my second year in college, I'd gained maturity and caught up to the others. God has a plan for our lives. He allows trials in order to make us better people, but unlike my coach, he won't banish us out of His sight.

Whatever happens in life to sack us, we must get up, learn from our mistakes, and move on. Failures shouldn't be paralyzers. Just as the Lord promises that nothing can keep us from the love of God, nothing should keep us from reaching the best plans He has for us.

Scheme

A term used to describe offensive and defensive game
plan and the overall strategy for an upcoming opponent.

Have a plan," Bret Bielema, my college coach, said. "Know what
works and go with that."

In my first couple of years of college, my biggest battle was to
quickly adjust to a new schedule and then plan. In football the schedule changes—camp, off-season workouts, regular season, traveling for
games, meetings. I had to become a creature of habit with what worked
for each season.

In the NFL, Houston's heat was a factor. First thing in the morning, a hard lift would cause my blood sugar to crash, so I'd rest for 30
minutes before going on a run. Then I had to eat so I didn't crash after
running.

Through trial and error I figured out what worked to get through a
game and what didn't. Complex carbs early in the morning and then
simpler carbs later—like a peanut butter sandwich on wheat bread—
kept me level and stable.

*Suppose one of you wants to build a tower. Won't you first
sit down and estimate the cost to see if you have enough
money to complete it? For if you lay the foundation and are
not able to finish it, everyone who sees it will ridicule you,
saying, "This person began to build and wasn't able to finish." Or suppose a king is about to go to war against another
king. Won't he first sit down and consider whether he is able
with ten thousand men to oppose the one coming against
him with twenty thousand? If he is not able, he will send a
delegation while the other is still a long way off and will ask
for terms of peace. In the same way, those of you who do not*

give up everything you have cannot be my disciples (Luke
14:28-33).

Diabetes is a battle, as is football and life. Going into a battle, you'll lose without a plan. Coaches always have a plan for the game. They don't understand diabetes but are concerned with my performance. My performance affects their performance, so they want me to be at the top of my game and have a plan, like Coach Bielema said.

Through high school, college, and the NFL, coaches counted on me to figure out what I needed to do regarding my diabetes in order to play football. I can't go in the game and say, "Well, I hope it's good today."

You have to have a scheme, a plan. The Bible tells us to have a plan too. What are you trying to build? What are you trying to accomplish? What battle are you facing? Do you have a scheme that will get you where you need to go?

Shift

When a team changes its alignment
before the ball is snapped.

In a hotel room before a Texans regular season game, my teammate pointed to the Bible and said, "Sometimes people put money in the Bible. Go ahead. Check it out."

I thought it odd but opened up the Bible to its middle, landing in the Psalms. "Before we look for money, shouldn't we read a verse or two?"

My teammate nodded and sat on the bed. I flipped to Psalm 81, since that was my number.

> Sing for joy to God our strength; shout aloud to the God of Jacob! (Psalm 81:1).

With my name being Jacob, God had my attention. I read on about all of the great things God had done for His people. Then a verse gave a warning. "Hear me, my people, and I will warn you" (Psalm 81:8). I looked up at my teammate, still listening attentively. I returned to the Holy Book, reading about how God would take care of us if we follow His ways and listen to Him. The psalm ended with God feeding us with the finest of wheat and honey from a rock (verse 16).

I took money from my wallet and placed it in the Bible. My friend did the same.

Sometimes God makes us shift our thinking. We were looking for money, but God gave us His Word, which was worth more than any amount of money. The message of Psalm 81 was about shifting our thinking back to God. He was telling us that He is our strength and we should be happy. He's also warning us not to turn against Him or things could go wrong. What more could we want to find when opening a Bible?

In a football game, we often shift. We give a different look right before the game. I may shift or trade, as some teams would say, from one side of the formation to the other. This could give us an advantage and make the execution of the play a little easier against the defense. Life can be the same. Sometimes we need to shift our attitude and thinking to make things work a little better, and sometimes God instructs us to shift. We need to be ready when He does.

Sideline

The line along each side of the field that marks
where the field of play ends and where players
stand behind, anxiously waiting to go in.

At the end of a season, while watching film with Danny Woodhead, Eric Weddle said, "Stop. Rewind." The San Diego Chargers special teams coach went back to where the camera was panned onto the sidelines, where a player went out of bounds. "Wait. Go back. Okay. Look at that." One of the defensive backs was doing handstands and clapping his feet together, playing around on the sidelines. We all died laughing while the coach replayed the tape again and again.

A cheerful heart is good medicine, but a crushed spirit dries up the bones (Proverbs 17:22).

Watching game film can be tense and drawn out, especially when you watch about six hours or more of film a day for seven months. You get sick of it. Toward the end of the season, guys get beat up and beat down. It helped to take our eyes off the field and look at a little sideline humor.

Worry and intensity and taking life too seriously dries up the bones. When Eric took a lighthearted look at the game film, we all had a good laugh and the tension drained away. Sometimes you need to take your eyes off what's in front of you to see the interesting activities on the sidelines. Lighten up! A sense of humor is God-given and should be used often in life.

Skill Set

The unique and individual abilities each player on
a team brings to the group. When constructing
a team, the general manager looks for every
skill set available to create the team.

During off-season for the Chargers, I took a break with some buddies
and went snowboarding on Big Bear Mountain, which is north of
San Diego. I'd only tried snowboarding once before, seven years earlier. My friends were avid and skilled snowboarders. We all rode the lift
together and they jumped off at the most difficult slope on the mountain. I didn't want to get lost from the group, so I followed.

At the top of the hill, my three friends started their descent. My
palms began to sweat inside my gloves. What had I gotten myself into?
My heart pounded against my chest. As they flew down the steep
mountain like birds taking flight, I said a prayer and went for it. Fail-
ing was not an option.

At the bottom of the hill, they turned and I stopped right beside
them.

"I'm sorry, Jake," Chris said, patting me on the back. "We forgot
you've never done this before."

"I can't believe you stayed with us," Max said.

"It's because he's a skilled athlete." Chris laughed. "C'mon, let's do
it again."

> *We have different gifts, according to the grace given to each*
> *of us. If your gift is prophesying, then prophesy in accordance*
> *with your faith; if it is serving, then serve; if it is teaching,*
> *then teach; if it is to encourage, then give encouragement;*
> *if it is giving, then give generously; if it is to lead, do it dili-*
> *gently; if it is to show mercy, do it cheerfully...Each of you*

*should use whatever gift you have received to serve others, as
faithful stewards of God's grace in its various forms (Romans
12:6-8; 1 Peter 4:10).*

In football, the offense is the hope and action. It makes the big
plays. Each person on the offense has a unique talent set that helps the
team score points. But the team needs not only skilled players, kick-
ers, and larger-than-life lineman, but also defensive-minded individuals who can launch their bodies into another human with abandon. All
the players are athletic and bring different skill sets to create one team.

Our God-given talent makes us who we are and sets us apart from
others. In the body of Christ, each person has a skill set that counts in
the game of life. There are no insignificant people in the offensive line,
defensive line, or in the body of Christ.

Talents are like muscles for an athlete. If not used, they won't grow
and strengthen. Being in optimum shape—and God's grace—helped
me take the steepest mountain at Big Bear and get to the bottom still
standing. If you keep your talents sharpened, you can optimize them
to get anywhere in life.

Everyone has a different set of talents—a God-given skill set—for
a purpose. Be confident in your skills, get into your position, and use
what you have to achieve success in all you do.

Snap Count

The numbers or words a quarterback shouts while waiting for the ball to be snapped. The quarterback usually informs his teammates in the huddle that the ball will be snapped on a certain count.

At recess in Rome, New York, my classmates and I waited in turn to fly down the hill. But this ride had rules and order. First, you had to get on the sled, then get in position, and then wait for the count. One. Two. Three. Then the next two students in line would give the push.

Wanting to show off when my turn came, I didn't wait for the count. I flung myself onto the sled on the top of the hill. But, stuck on wet snow, it didn't move even though I did. I rode my face the entire way down.

Pride brings a person low, but the lowly in spirit gain honor (Proverbs 29:23).

My pride brought me low that day. At the bottom of the hill, my face burned with both hill rash and embarrassment. In football, if players don't wait for the count, there's a penalty, either "offsides" or "false start," depending on if you're ahead of or behind the ball. It's embarrassing, especially when it happens in front of 80,000 fans and a television audience.

There's order to everything on a team. The game is never a one-man show. You have to wait for the quarterback to give you the snap count. It's like that in life too. I wore the scars from that incident for a while to remind me of my lack of listening skills.

After being brought low, we can regain our honor and learn to listen to God's count. Sometimes our timing isn't right. When we wait for God to count… "One. Two. Three. Now go!" we won't land on our face in an embarrassing and painful situation.

129

Special Teams

Special teams make up the third component of the
football team, aside from offense and defense.
Special teams play in all the kickoffs, both as the
kicking as well as the receiving team. Special
teams can sometimes give a player who may be
a backup an opportunity to gain playing time.

When Wisconsin Badgers head coach Bret Bielema offered me a full scholarship, he said, "I'm not going to promise you the world, but I will promise you an opportunity. It won't be easy, but what you accomplish is up to you."

In the height of recruitment, promises from coaches were coming at me left and right. Recruiting coaches are like used car salesmen when trying to get players to come to their school, but Coach Bielema's words rang the most sincere. All I ever wanted was an opportunity to work toward success.

> *Be very careful, then, how you live—not as unwise but as wise, making the most of every opportunity, because the days are evil (Ephesians 5:15-16).*

In my freshman year at the University of Wisconsin, I sure did think the times were evil because of the difficulties that came my way— managing college, football, and diabetes—but I had an opportunity with my football scholarship. Another opportunity came my way when Coach Bielema put me on special teams.

No matter how minimal special teams may be to the average spectator, that was an important part of my college career. Special teams provide an opportunity to catch the eye of a coach you may impress enough to earn more serious playing time on either the offense or defense.

I grabbed that opportunity and worked hard. Bret Bielema assured me he was confident that in every game I'd get my job done. In those years—2008 to 2011—we had a great group of players, maybe the best offense in the nation. I finished my college career playing in back-to-back Rose Bowl games.

What are your talents? What opportunities have you been given, and what have you done with them? What can you still do? God gives everyone talents, and opportunities will come your way. Be prepared to make the most of them.

Strip

When the defender grabs or knocks the ball out of an opponent's hands. When recovered by the defensive team, a swing of momentum ensues along with a hopeful advantage that the recovering team can score.

At Rogers High School in Arkansas, I covered the football field, playing offense and defense. I was strong enough to control the line and fast enough to catch any running back from behind. I also anchored the line and collapsed my side so opposing teams could never rush for more than three yards.

During the fourth quarter, the game was going great...until a wrong answer to my coach's question got me benched and caused a loss for the team.

I had a headache due to high blood sugar and asked the coach for an aspirin.

My coach didn't know anything about diabetes and assumed I'd gotten hit on the field.

"Do you remember getting hit?"

"No."

The answer I gave was right, but wrong. I didn't remember getting hit because I wasn't hit. The coach wouldn't put me back in the game. From the sidelines, I watched the other team rush for 250 yards in the second half and a score a field goal in the final seconds.

> *Everyone must submit to governing authorities. For all authority comes from God, and those in positions of authority have been placed there by God (Romans 13:1 NLT).*

That day I was so frustrated with the coach's decision to pull me. I wanted to plead my case. Watching the team lose hurt more than my initial headache.

Concussions are a huge worry in football and coaches always want to err on the side of caution. I learned two things during that game: to be careful with my words and accept the decision by authorities. Maybe for reasons unknown to me, I needed to sit out the rest of the game.

Sometimes, when life deals you a blow, it seems as if God is stripping something from your hands. Losses come in many forms, but ultimately He is the coach over our life. Whatever we speak in prayer, God won't get confused. He understands our hearts. If He pulls us out of a game, maybe it's for a good reason. The important thing is that we can always trust Him both with things lost and the wonderful things He gives us.

Stunts

When a lineman goes in a different direction than the opposing player expects him to, and the linebacker replaces him at his position. It's used to blitz, confuse, and fool the offensive blocking assignments.

On a rare day off during Chargers camp in my second year in the NFL, I scrambled out of bed with a million things on my mental to-do list. First priority: haircut.

I stepped into the hair salon closest to my apartment and followed the hairdresser, a Korean lady, to her booth. I couldn't understand her broken English but figured I didn't need to understand her to get a simple haircut.

She shook out the cape, put it around me, and asked a question. With her accent, I had no idea what she asked. Probably catching my quizzical look, she smiled, nodded, and said, "You like. Okay?"

I shrugged. "Okay."

After the shampoo, she threw another non-English question at me. Again, when I didn't understand, she nodded, smiled, and said, "You like. Okay?"

The appointment continued like that. I'd nod in agreement each time with no idea what I was agreeing to. I ended up with a scalp massage and then hair treatments. She even straightened my already straight hair. I said I didn't need it, but she insisted.

I'd had enough. I texted my fiancée to come rescue me. She was close by and within a few minutes, she entered the salon and discovered me trapped under a tiny helmet dryer, wearing a hairnet.

"What are you doing?" Emma asked.

"I don't know. I don't speak Korean."

The hairdresser came at me, wearing gloves and carrying foil.

"He doesn't need highlights." Emma tugged me out of the chair.

*Then we will no longer be infants, tossed back and forth
by the waves, and blown here and there by every wind of
teaching and by the cunning and craftiness of people in their
deceitful scheming (Ephesians 4:14).*

That hair appointment cost me more than a hundred dollars. If Emma hadn't shown up, there's no telling what the final charge would have been. I had a sneaking suspicion that lady knew what she was doing, smiling and using affirming words to trick me into getting much more than a simple haircut.

As an offensive player, we use trickery in our calls all the time. The quarterback will yell his cadence when we line up on the ball and throw in dummy words with our real signals that actually have no meaning. This is done in hopes that the defensive team would think they understood what is being said and change their plans, when in actuality the words they thought they understood meant nothing at all.

To survive in the NFL, we have to be smart. In any situation, we need to be vigilant. As Christians, if we are sharp and mature, we won't be tossed back and forth by the waves, accepting any new teaching that comes along. We run into all types of people, talking about things we may not understand. There's too much crazy stuff in the world. We have to be careful and stick with the truths that God teaches in Scripture so we don't get led down a wrong pathway. We should never agree to things we don't really understand, like me—a helpless man in a beauty salon, held captive by a hairdresser. It's always better to surround ourselves with people who speak the truth, are up front, and aren't out to trick us. It's also important to always have that one person you can trust and lean on to help you through certain unexpected situations.

Take a Knee

If the ball goes deep into the end zone, and the
defensive players are swarming and closing in
on the player who caught it in the end zone, then
he may "take a knee" to indicate the ball is down,
the play is over, and the referee will place the
ball on the 20 yard line for the first down of the
new possession. That's called a "touchback."

I took out my cell and called my mom as I walked back to my dorm. "If I failed this test, I'm done."

"Pray," she said. She assured me of her prayers.

In my second semester at the University of Wisconsin, I had too much on my plate and was not balancing my life well. When I got to my room I tossed my backpack onto my bed. If I failed the test, which I probably did, I'd be kicked off the team. The coach had warned me. We had a great shot at a bowl game, and I'd messed up my life and consequently my chances of continuing to play football besides the thrill of experiencing a postseason game. Best scenario, I could rejoin the team after I got my grades up.

Feeling as if a slew of mighty defensive players were about to slam into me, I took a knee at the edge of my bed and asked God for help, promising I'd get my act together. Next, I emailed the teacher and my academic advisor, explaining my situation.

Reform your ways and your actions and obey the LORD your God. Then the LORD will relent and not bring the disaster he has pronounced against you (Jeremiah 26:13).

I rejoiced, earning a D on that test. While still not great, it was all I needed to pass. I got a lecture from my coach, but he gave me a little leeway since I'd done better during the first semester.

When we've really messed things up and disaster is about to land upon us, it's often our own fault. Best we can do is turn to God, do what we can do to remedy the situation, and then move on, keeping our promise to change our ways.

After taking a knee and making promises to God and a lot of other people—parents, coaches, advisor—I had to do the right things going forward and reform my ways. I did. And looking back, I can see how God really blessed me.

Tandem Block

Two offensive players blocking one guy, normally
double-teaming a defensive lineman up to a linebacker.

In college, my friend Blake and I bought a tandem bike to ride together to practice. When we weren't overwhelmed with football and school, we'd ride up and down sorority row jamming to Vanessa Carlton's "A Thousand Miles" blaring from the portable speakers we hooked up in our little basket. Our hope was to get noticed by the ladies.

After this the LORD appointed seventy-two others and sent them two by two ahead of him to every town and place where he was about to go (Luke 10:1).

Tandem bike rides with Blake helped to cut the stress of a rigorous schedule. On the field, working in tandem works great against the best players. Two can always get the job done where one might fail. Certainly, the Lord knew that two were better than one. I'll bet those 72 disciples, as they went out evangelizing two by two, shared smiles and laughter along the way. Maybe even a little singing.

Going at it alone can lead you down a road to failure, no matter what tunes you're jamming to along the way. In football, you need your brother. Your team becomes your extended family, and working together helps everyone achieve their goals. The better the lineman, normally, the better the running back. A great receiver can make the quarterback all-pro. The defensive line can keep the blockers off the linebackers so they can make all, if not most of the tackles, and two defensive backs can take the best receiver out of the game.

So don't tough things out by yourself. You'll get where you're going faster, and in a better mood, when you team up with a wingman.

Tight End

A versatile position that is like a combination between an offensive lineman and a wide receiver. Tight ends can align on the line of scrimmage next to an offensive tackle and assist in blocking schemes or they can run a route. They can also split out to become a receiver.

My position, tight end, is like the Swiss army knife of the offense. The tight end has to be able to do many things on the field—blocker, receiver, and even running back in some protections, so you need to know the positions on the offense, not just one spot. And depending on different packages, sometimes you're in as fullback or as a wide receiver, and sometimes you're running down the field to catch a ball, monitoring to run a route, or lead-blocking for a run play. To be a tight end, you have to be versatile.

In high school, I got just as many offers from college coaches to play defensive end as I did tight end. But I loved the versatility of the offensive positon and chose to remain in that.

> *Though I am free and belong to no one, I have made myself a slave to everyone, to win as many as possible. To the Jews I became like a Jew, to win the Jews. To those under the law I became like one under the law (though I myself am not under the law), so as to win those under the law. To those not having the law I became like one not having the law (though I am not free from God's law but am under Christ's law), so as to win those not having the law. To the weak I became weak, to win the weak. I have become all things to all people so that by all possible means I might save some. I do all this for the sake of the gospel, that I may share in its blessings (1 Corinthians 9:19-23).*

In the Bible, Paul had to be versatile to win souls for Christ, but he never lost his identity as a Christian. He knew who he was in Christ.

In life, being able to step into different roles is key to success, but we can't go against the rules or laws in being all things to all people. While I play a versatile position, I must stay within the rules of the game.

Use the gifts God has given you and be willing to step outside your comfort zone while remaining within the parameters of God's laws. Be a versatile player for Him. Understand who you are, and confidently live the life He has planned for you.

Time-Out

A legal pause in the action of the game. Each
team is allowed three time-outs per half and
can use them when they wish to stop the clock.
Officials can also call time-outs to measure first
down yardage or if a player is injured.

I'd played basketball for years, but after my diabetes diagnosis I took time off from the sport. I'd lost so much weight that I had to take a step back and focus on getting strong again for football and figure out how to manage my disease.

Several of my buddies also quit the basketball team that year to focus on weight gain for the next football season. But we all missed the sport and decided to join a youth center team just for fun. Three of us were starters on the high school basketball team. We played against recreational players—older guys and younger ones who didn't make the school team—and went undefeated. Each game, we ran onto the court with one goal in mind—to have fun. Not only did we win games, we were also benched with the most technical fouls out of any team. The basketball refs hated to see us and would constantly yell at us to be more serious players.

We'd do crazy things. I'd get down on all fours and one player would jump on my back and dunk the ball. We even pulled out the barking play, where two of us would get on all fours and bark like dogs to distract the players while another player scored.

> *Be joyful at your festival—you, your sons and daughters,*
> *your male and female servants, and the Levites, the foreign-*
> *ers, the fatherless and the widows who live in your towns.*
> *For seven days celebrate the festival to the LORD your God*
> *at the place the LORD will choose. For the LORD your God*

will bless you in all your harvest and in all the work of
your hands, and your joy will be complete (Deuteronomy
16:14-15).

In the book of Deuteronomy, God sets aside times of festivals—designated fun times meant to be a break from the seriousness of life. He wants us to be joyful people. Jesus was known to attend banquets and weddings, and He even turned water into wine. We have to live in this world and be effective to Christ, but we also need to be out among people and having fun too.

With all the heavy diabetes stuff, I needed a respite. Highly regulated high school basketball didn't allow for the fun and crazy stunts my buddies and I pulled. There are times when we have to be serious—like football season—and times we need a break to refresh ourselves and have a little fun playing a sport.

An occasional break from the seriousness of life can make all the difference in how joyful you are.

Touchdown

When the ball carrier reaches the end zone and
crosses the goal line, it results in a six-point score.

At the University of Wisconsin, as a tight end my strong skill set was blocking, so I didn't often get balls thrown my way. But every game I'd suit up and pray that pigskin would graciously fall into my well-deserving arms.

"I'll try to get the ball in your hands today, Jake." Quarterback Scott Tolzien patted my back as we headed onto home field to play Indiana during our junior year. He and other teammates knew how badly I wanted that first college touchdown and would encourage me prior to each game.

During the second quarter, even though I wasn't even open, Scott lasered the ball straight to me. I caught it and ran the two yards into the end zone. Touchdown! A slew of Badgers jumped on my back, clashed helmets against mine, and offered congratulatory pats on my shoulder. A shared victory.

> As long as Moses held up his hands, the Israelites were winning, but whenever he lowered his hands, the Amalekites were winning (Exodus 17:11)

In the book of Exodus, the Bible tells how, as long as Moses raised his staff, the Israelites prevailed in battle against the Amalekites. When his arms grew tired and his staff fell, the Amalekites gained ground. Aaron and Hur, after discussing strategy, supported Moses's arms until the battle was won. Ultimately, it was God who brought about the win, but with support of the entire army, and Aaron and Hur's intervention, the Israelites saw victory. Teamwork won the day.

Scott Tolzien's pass led me to a victorious touchdown in the end zone. With the teamwork of the entire offense, I earned my first collegiate touchdown. The team celebrated. Victory is never achieved alone.

It's like that in life too. No victory happens by a solitary action. God makes a way for us to be victorious, but we need helpers. And in life, as in football, the enemy engages us at every turn.

Jesus Christ will lead us victoriously to heaven at the end zone of our life, but it will take the body of Christ to remain united and strong so we can win daily earthly battles. I imagine when we rush through the gates of heaven, those who have helped us will be there, celebrating our victory.

Touchdown Dance

A player's celebration of his touchdown catch
in the end zone. Spiking the ball and some
dance moves are allowed, but not other stuff
the NFL deems as excessive celebration.

Got your end zone show planned for your first touchdown?"

Seated on the couch in my San Diego apartment, I caught the football my brother Nick tossed to me. He'd come for a visit prior to our football camps—his as a Ragin' Cajun tight end in college and mine as an NFL Chargers tight end.

"You gotta have swag and set your own style, you know. Like Terrell Owens when he carried a Sharpie in his sock, signed the ball, and threw it to the fans."

"That's illegal now." Football in hand, I leaped off the couch. "How about this?" I busted out in a smooth dance move and then spiked the ball.

"Too complicated." Nick laughed. "Too bad you're not playing for the Packers. It'd be easy to do the Lambeau Leap into the stands. Just don't be a copycat and do the dirty bird or pretend to make a cell phone call. Those are done."

Coached by Nick, I perfected a simple but signature dance move.

A couple of months later, during the second preseason game against the Seattle Seahawks, at the end of the fourth quarter, Coach called a time-out and the play that would send me into the end zone to catch a touchdown pass. The play down, the end zone dance in my head, I geared up for my big moment.

Everything went as planned. I released as if to block and the defense took the fake hook, line, and sinker. I was unaccounted for. In this preseason game, the Seahawks had me marked only as a blocker. I ran my route as Kellen Clemens lobbed the ball toward me.

Perfect catch!

Touchdown!

Stunned and in awe, I froze. Zach Boren, a teammate who was also with me on the Texans, jumped all over me. Everyone was hopping up and down, attacking me. I thanked God and looked at the ball. Still in my hands.

Signature dance move! Gotta do it.

It was too late. I couldn't remember the moves Nick taught me. I tried a sorry attempt of a power spike and ran off the field. Still flying high and flustered, I forgot to run out for the next play. If not for the two-minute warning, I would have received a penalty.

> *After six days Jesus took with him Peter, James and John the brother of James, and led them up a high mountain by themselves. There he was transfigured before them. His face shone like the sun, and his clothes became as white as the light. Just then there appeared before them Moses and Elijah, talking with Jesus. Peter said to Jesus, "Lord, it is good for us to be here. If you wish, I will put up three shelters—one for you, one for Moses and one for Elijah" (Matthew 17:1-4).*

I had the sequence planned out for my touchdown, but stunned and caught up in the moment like Peter, I forget my end zone dance. Only the glory of the moment mattered.

Standing before the Son of God, Elijah (a great prophet), and Moses (the lawgiver), Peter wanted to build a tent and stay, not realizing the moment would be fleeting. I understand that. Entranced in my moment of glory and overpowered by the immensity of the experience, I didn't want to leave the field.

Peter's amazing experience was so much greater than my touchdown moment, but definitely both were moments in which God blessed us. During times in your life where God's grace is evident, revel in the moment and thank Him, but don't forget that when the moment ends you have to get back to reality to avoid a penalty.

Trainer

Athletic trainers are a part of the immediate field-side medical staff who assist the team's medical needs. They work with the team doctors and also help keep players hydrated and stretched.

The athletic trainer tossed me a Powerade. He'd just checked my blood sugar levels and I was a little low.

"I'll check again at halftime."

He moved on down the bench and taped up a teammate's ankle. An assistant trainer gave a player a bottle of water. An intern massaged the muscles of a lineman.

> *Then the devil left him, and angels came and attended him (Matthew 4:11).*

Within every team is a team of athletic trainers: the head trainer, assistants, and interns. They are visible angels on the sidelines, helping players and dealing with injuries. In Houston, playing for the Texans, the team had a paramedic who always took special care of me on game day.

Visible helpers not only deal with our physical ailments but also give us a sense of comfort. Jesus is our invisible helper. Though we don't see Him, He is right next to us, cheering for us through good times, supporting us through difficult times, and whispering wisdom, insight, and directions in all of life's arenas.

Also on God's team are helpers in the form of angels, like the ones who helped Jesus after the devil tested Him in the desert. He'd fasted for 40 days and nights and was put through several tests. The Bible references angels helping people or coming to give news to people. It even says that sometimes when we entertain strangers, we are unaware that we are entertaining angels (Hebrews 13:1-2).

We should always be grateful for the seen and unseen angels around us.

Trash Talk

Comments one player will make to another player
of the opposing team in hopes of intimidating
to gain advantage.

Y ou're nothing but a hick from Arkansas. A fat, stupid hick. You're
a piece of trash."

Back in Arkansas, I was on a big high school stage and playing for
the largest conference, sometimes in front of more than 5,000 fans. But
it was nothing compared to getting trashed by fans in an arena of more
than 100,000 fans, especially when they have obviously read your bio
and found a trash talking point. I learned to deal with it—just smile
and wave to the fans who cursed me.

I've had my share of smack talk on the field. Not a big deal. Often
opposing players would growl and threaten me or say something derog-
atory about my mother. When insulted, I learned that the best defense
is to ignore the mother comments, and for the other comments, wink,
smile, and say something back like, "I love it when you talk dirty to me."

> *The men who were guarding Jesus began mocking and beat-
> ing him. They blindfolded him and demanded, "Prophesy!
> Who hit you?" And they said many other insulting things to
> him (Luke 22:63-65).*

In the Bible, on the night of Jesus's passion, He took a lot of abuse,
even turning the other cheek. And it got worse. The people Jesus came
to save rejected Him and sent Him to a death on a cross after beat-
ings, scourging with a nailed whip, gouges with long sharp thorns, and
punches with fists.

Look to Jesus and how He handled His crucifixion. The best thing
we can do when mocked or taunted is to either douse it with humor
or turn the other cheek.

Turnover

The loss of the ball via a fumble or an interception.

During my freshman year of college, I was a jerk, cursing like an idiot and trying my best to be a tough football player. I did a lot of dumb things that, if not for the grace of God, could have gotten me kicked off the team or even worse. My girlfriend from high school, attending college with me, dumped me. She said I wasn't the same guy she once knew. She was right but I didn't listen.

A few days after my girlfriend broke up with me, I was at a party and one of my teammates mouthed off to a guy bigger than him. The guy responded by punching him in the face. Before I could step in and break up the fight, my friend had been beaten so badly that I had to take him to the hospital. He ended up having surgery and lost his place on the team.

> *You were taught, with regard to your former way of life, to put off your old self, which is being corrupted by its deceitful desires; to be made new in the attitude of your minds; and to put on the new self, created to be like God in true righteousness and holiness (Ephesians 4:22-24).*

Unable to sleep after leaving my friend in the hospital, I tossed and turned. When the sun came up, I stared at my dorm room ceiling. The way I'd been acting lately, I could have been in the same position as my friend. Other party situations could have cost me a lot. Who was I? Not that idiot going down the wrong pathway. Had I come to Wisconsin to play football and get a degree or to party? I'd fumbled and fallen into a situation that wasn't going to have a good outcome. I needed to change my attitude or I was going to jeopardize my football career, my future, and maybe my life.

A turnover in football means you've lost the ball and the other team has an opportunity to take over. If I failed, God could choose someone else to do what He'd chosen me to do. I'd fumbled, had a turnover. A turnover in football is bad. A turnover in life is good. I needed the good kind of a turnover.

That morning, I turned myself over to God, thanking Him for keeping me out of trouble and asking for forgiveness. I asked Him to guide me on a better path.

Because of the sacrifice Jesus made for us on the cross, when we've made mistakes we can always ask for forgiveness, get back up, and remind ourselves to put off our old selves and put on the new.

It takes bravery to walk away from a lifestyle that ultimately hurts you, makes you weak, and has the potential to destroy. But when we turn ourselves over to God and ask Him to change us, a transformation takes place. The Bible calls it a "renewing of the mind" (Romans 12:2). You will still be you, but you will be better. You will be a stronger and wiser version of yourself.

For me, staying on the right path is a daily effort. Are you going down a wrong path? Maybe it's time to put off your old self, turn yourself over to God, and take on a new attitude.

Two-Minute Warning

A stop in the game clock two minutes before each half. Normally results in a TV commercial.

et's get him suited up!" I could hear the excitement in the coach's voice. The beaming smile on my dad's face and the pat on my back told me expectations were high that day, my first year of tackle football. I was in the third grade in Marshall, Michigan.

I was at my awkward chubby stage and kept falling over my huge feet during the drills. The coach was pushing me, my dad was pushing me, and the sun beat down on me.

I hated football.

I constantly got yelled at for messing up. My dad and the coaches thought that because I was bigger and stronger than the other kids, I should be a better player. But I hadn't grown into my body yet. Though I wanted to quit, my dad forced me to play out the season.

There is a time for everything, and a season for every activity under the heavens (Ecclesiastes 3:1).

The two-minute warning is a time for the team to regroup. I needed two years to regroup and figure out if I would continue to play the sport. Toward the end of the next summer, with disappointments and bad memories of the past season lingering in my mind, I didn't want to play football. My dad, though not happy, didn't force me to play.

The following year, we moved to Rogers, Arkansas. With the changing of the seasons, there was a buzz in the neighborhood about youth football. Everyone was signing up.

"You're bigger than anyone." My friend Anthony Stobaugh shot a basket into the net in the driveway. "You have to sign up."

Knowing all my friends would be playing youth football, I decided to give it a try again. I'd changed a lot in two years and had a different attitude. I was ready.

I rebounded the ball. "I'll do it!"

Turned out to be the right decision. The right time.

When pushing ourselves, or when someone else is pushing us to do something and it doesn't work out, don't count it as a failure. Don't give up.

Is there anything that you gave up on because of poor results, thinking you weren't good at it? Have you given it a season of rest? Maybe it's time to try again.

Unit

A group of players that plays every down next to
each other. A close, bonded 11-man unit that has
each other's back on the field no matter what.

During the 2014 training camp for the San Diego Chargers, running back Danny Woodhead, who was always sporting his best effort at facial hair, said, "Let's all unite. Shave everything but our moustaches and have a contest for the best moustache at the end of camp. Who's in?"

"I'm in." I'd had my beard since joining professional football.

"Count me in." Philip Rivers rubbed his chin. Though he didn't have a beard, he said he'd be glad to take the challenge and grow a 'stache.

"We'll call it Camp Rally 'Stache," Danny said.

Shaving off our facial hair except for our moustache became a uniting objective, something to get our minds off the difficulties of camp and to have a little fun.

Finally, all of you, have unity of mind, sympathy, brotherly love, a tender heart, and a humble mind (1 Peter 3:8 ESV).

Giving up all facial hair except for the Camp Rally 'Stache wasn't a huge sacrifice, but it was a show of unity. This situation reminded me of a time during one high school football camp when my teammates and I all had our heads shaved into Mohawks.

People show a united front by wearing pink for breast cancer awareness or flying banners or flags. The Bible is full of verses that call us to unite, one to another, and using a sign or a symbol helps the cause. Early Christians embraced a fish symbol and Christians today use that symbol and the cross to identify our faith. The Bible says to unite in brotherly love. Symbols and signs of unity are great, but the most important sign is the one that should identify Christians—how we love one another.

Waived

During the first four years of a rookie contract, a player can get waived or cut. At that time, the player hits the waiver wire and is available to be picked up by any of the other 31 teams.

We had you on the ready list," said Gary Kubiak, head coach of the Texans. He'd picked me up from the San Diego Chargers practice squad when one of his tight ends got hurt. Prior to that I'd been on the New Orleans Saints and played in a preseason game against the Texans.

From high school football onward, I knew other coaches kept me on their radar. That makes the pressure huge to perform. Through college, I had to bear in mind that NFL coaches might be watching.

Now, in the NFL, every game is a résumé. You aren't just playing for your team; you're playing for all 32 teams. You never know when you might get cut and be on the radar of other teams.

You have searched me, LORD, and you know me. You know when I sit and when I rise; you perceive my thoughts from afar. You discern my going out and my lying down; you are familiar with all my ways. Before a word is on my tongue you, LORD, know it completely. You hem me in behind and before, and you lay your hand upon me. Such knowledge is too wonderful for me, too lofty for me to attain. Where can I go from your Spirit? Where can I flee from your presence? If I go up to the heavens, you are there; if I make my bed in the depths, you are there. If I rise on the wings of the dawn, if I settle on the far side of the sea, even there your hand will guide me, your right hand will hold me fast (Psalm 139:1-10).

Football players are watched. And if you are really good, you are watched by college coaches and then NFL coaches. Knowing you're observed, you have to make a concentrated effort to do your very best.

Consider your life a football field where God—the Head Coach above all coaches, the Lord of all lords, and King of all kings—watches. Shouldn't we be constantly aware and striving toward peak performance to be the best Christian in all areas of our lives? Coaches may judge and determine the future of a football player, but Jesus judges us and determines our place for all eternity. We ought to be doing our best to earn a crown in heaven, which is greater than any trophy earned on earth.

Walk-On

An opportunity for a high school player to be a part of a
college football program and earn a spot on the team.

During halftime at a Michigan State basketball game, while wearing our team sweats, I hobbled out onto the court with the help of a pair of crutches—something I had found backstage and decided on the spur of the moment to use for effect. When Miley Cyrus's "Party in the USA" blasted from speakers, I flung the crutches across the gym floor, grabbed my partner, and led nine teammates in a dance routine.

> *Whoever watches the wind will not plant; whoever looks at the clouds will not reap. As you do not know the path of the wind, or how the body is formed in a mother's womb, so you cannot understand the work of God, the Maker of all things. Sow your seed in the morning, and at evening let your hands not be idle, for you do not know which will succeed, whether this or that, or whether both will do equally well (Ecclesiastes 11:4-6).*

Every year the University of Wisconsin dance team picks ten football players to learn a dance for the biggest rival basketball game of the season. Ten out of our most ungraceful oafs worked out for weeks to master our routine.

Even walk-ons in college football can go on to the NFL. J.J. Watt, my teammate on the Wisconsin Badgers, was a walk-on. He was drafted and became 2013 Associated Press NFL Defensive Player of the Year.

My "walk-on" on the basketball court to begin a dance routine didn't earn me any awards or accolades, but we made ESPN's SportCenter's "Not Top 10" list. We rocked that performance and thought it would be a YouTube sensation after appearing on ESPN, but we were disappointed when we only had a few hits.

Succeeding in life is about taking chances, no matter the outcome. Like the book of Ecclesiastes says, you just can't watch the wind. We don't always know God's plan for us, but stepping out, taking a chance, and pushing beyond comfort zones to do something out of the ordinary and unexpected can lead to new experiences.

Weak Side

The side of the offense opposite the side
on which the tight end lines up.

In the third grade I lived in upstate New York, and every day in the winter we packed our snow gear—snow pants, gloves, and hat. Getting ready for school one morning, my mom used my nylon bag to pull clothes from the dryer. She dumped the clothes in another basket and stuck in my snow gear required for recess.

Later at school when the recess bell rang, my classmates and I grabbed our bags from our lockers and returned to our desks to suit up for winter fun.

Standing by my desk in the classroom, I dumped out my bag, and my sister's pink underwear fell on top of my outdoor gear. My face turned red hot and I made a grab for them to shove them back into the bag. Too late. A kid next to me noticed them and chanted, "Jake wears pink undies." Everyone in the classroom laughed and chorused, "Jake wears pink undies." I wanted to crawl in a hole.

> The LORD is my light and my salvation—whom shall I fear?
> The LORD is the stronghold of my life—of whom shall I be
> afraid? When the wicked advance against me to devour me,
> it is my enemies and my foes who will stumble and fall.
> Though an army besiege me, my heart will not fear; though
> war break out against me, even then I will be confident
> (Psalm 27:1-3).

A weak side in football is the side opposite to where the tight end lines up. Being a tight end, I'm always on the strong side. But in life, and in the game, though we may feel we are in the perfect place, something can happen that strips away our confidence. We may make a dumb move, goof up, or just find ourselves the focus of a bad joke. What do you do? David, in the psalms, looked to God as his light and salvation. He was chosen by God to be the next king. David, the same guy who killed the giant Goliath with a slingshot, found himself running for his life in fear of Saul, who wanted to kill him. Who did he look to for help? God!

When we find ourselves in a precarious position, or just plain embarrassed and trying to hide a pair of pink undies, all we can do is look to God to be the strong side in our lives. He loves us no matter what.

Wedge-Buster

Players who run full speed, risking life and limb as they
hurl their bodies at the players making up the wedge
(a wall of players the return man screens behind).

On my fifteenth birthday, I didn't have a cake, I didn't have pizza, and I didn't have soda. I'd just been diagnosed with diabetes a few months earlier and was doing everything I could to control my insulin levels by staying away from carbs and sugar. I was determined to control diabetes and not let it get the best of me.

My football goals pushed me toward many sacrifices. I didn't want my disease to hold me back, so I took a shot of insulin in the morning and controlled diabetes the rest of the way with diet and exercise, making every sacrifice I could to maintain my sugar levels.

> *God so loved the world that he gave his one and only Son, that whoever believes in him shall not perish but have eternal life (John 3:16).*

Wedge-busters are the big guys on the team who hit and get hit with reckless abandon, sacrificing their bodies for the game. Each one is the man's man of the NFL. Yet no one knows more about sacrifice than Jesus. He is God, who became man for one purpose, to offer Himself for the sake of humanity.

I remember watching *The Passion of the Christ* with my throat tightening and my stomach tying up in knots. It was heart wrenching to watch the movie adaptation of the crucifixion of Christ, to see His broken, bloody figure on the cross. He was defeated but victorious. Tough movie to watch, but it sunk into my heart how His blood gave us the opportunity to be okay with God.

Jesus's sacrifice gained us salvation. Our sacrifices should be ones that get us closer to our goals. Sometimes not meeting goals means we didn't make the necessary sacrifices. By giving up cake, pizza, and soda on my birthday and every other day, I was able to maintain my sugar levels and stay in the game.

If Jesus could do what He did, with His help we should be able to make small sacrifices that help us reach our goals.

Wingback

A versatile playing position used for multiple roles on a play. The wingback is positioned one yard off the line of scrimmage and right outside the tight end. Depending on what play the coach calls, the wingback could be a running back, wide receiver, fullback, or a tight end.

In the church basement, my mom held out a pair of wings. "Please, Jake. Be an angel."

"C'mon, Mom. Those wings are for a little kid. I'm over six feet tall. This is ridiculous. Everyone will laugh at me."

Christmas Eve, at the little church where my stepfather pastored, I resented being forced into standing in for a no-show angel. It was *so* not cool. "I'll look like an overgrown angel dork." I crossed my arms. I'd done my best to ditch church and avoid singing Christmas carols in nursing homes, serving food to the poor, and other youth group activities. Being an angel in the Christmas play was the last thing I wanted to do on Christmas Eve.

"C'mon, Jake." My little brother tugged my arm. "Angel Gabriel is a big, powerful angel. He appears before Mary and scares her." Nick, dressed in his Joseph costume, looked toward my sister, playing Mary.

"You don't need a costume to look scary," Betsy said, pulling her blue shawl over her shoulders.

"Please." My mom handed me a white alb.

"Oh, all right." I pulled it on and sighed.

"It's just a few lines." My mom turned me around and fastened my wings. "You can read from the script."

A little while later, standing in the sanctuary, my sister whispered, "Jake!"

"Okay. Okay." I looked at the sheet and read with no enthusiasm, "Hail, Mary, full of grace. The Lord is with thee."

My sister, the drama queen, pressed her hand on her chest and looked really scared.

I grinned and looked down at my paper. "Don't be afraid, Mary. You have found favor with God. You will be with child and give birth to a Son, and you are to give Him the name Jesus. He will be great and will be called the Son of the Most High." I looked out into the church, filled with poinsettias and candles and low lights. Not a sound in the congregation. All eyes were on us.

It hit me. The people were here tonight because they wanted to hear this Good News, which was first said two thousand years ago and repeated now…by me. Chills ran down my arms.

I am not ashamed of the gospel, for it is the power of God for salvation to everyone who believes (Romans 1:16 ESV).

In football, a wingback can be used in many different ways. They sometimes confuse the defense because the opposing players must determine what the role of the wingback is for that particular play within a few seconds before the play starts. With the wingback able to block, handoff, or run downfield for a pass, there is room for the defense to lose sight of the ball and the wingback to take the team to victory with a touchdown.

That Christmas, though I was angry and embarrassed to put on a pair of wings and read the gospel, God spoke to my heart. I wasn't so important, but my words were. During the football season, I was a wingback on the field, and with the crowd watching, I ran the ball into the end zone, leading the team to a victory with a touchdown.

In a new position, I stood at the altar of God with the crowd in front of me waiting to hear God's Word. I finished reading from the script, adding more heart and sharing the Good News that leads all people to victory in Christ.

X-Receiver

The wide receiver who is considered one of
the team's biggest playmakers.

Sit out." My PE teacher tapped my shoulder as I was about to head
outside to join my classmates in a game of Ultimate Frisbee.

"Why, Coach?" My PE teacher was also my head football coach.

"You're my biggest playmaker in football, Jake. I can't risk having
you get hurt in PE class. Save your talents for Friday night."

Throughout the school year, I was often used as a wide receiver on
the field. Coach Peacock never let me participate in PE activities that
had potential to cause me an injury.

> *Each of you should use whatever gift you have received to
> serve others, as faithful stewards of God's grace in its vari-
> ous forms (1 Peter 4:10).*

Everyone counts on the X-receiver to make the big play. Coach Peacock protected me during PE class so I wouldn't get hurt, so I could
make the big plays in football because that's where my talents lie.

God wants us to make big plays for His team. As our Head Coach
in life, He values the gifts and talents He's given us and doesn't want us
to waste them foolishly or use them for the wrong purpose. Life is all
about how we use our talents to help others and glorify God.

Coach Peacock always stressed how much the team counted on me.
God counts on each of us to play out our roles in life. If compassion
is your talent, you might consider working in an area that serves others, like in the medical field. If you have a talent for reaching children,
teaching may be in your future.

Understanding our talents and respecting them helps us confidently make the big plays in life.

Yards After Catch

Yards gained after the receiver catches the ball.

When I was a little kid, convincing my mom to stop for a Happy Meal at McDonald's was like gaining yards after a catch. But as I grew, though Happy Meals were still the coolest thing after school, there came a time when they didn't fill me up. So I worked out a deal with my mom. Because my younger sister and brother got enough to eat, plus a toy, she agreed to buy me a 20-piece nugget meal and an additional cheeseburger and afterward, take me to Walmart for a small toy.

> *When I was a child, I spoke like a child, I thought like a child, I reasoned like a child. When I became a man, I gave up childish ways (1 Corinthians 13:11 ESV).*

When I was a child, I soon realized kids' meals wouldn't satisfy my appetite, but I still wanted the prize. As I matured, nutritious food mattered more than dessert or a toy, especially after I was diagnosed with diabetes. It's like that as we grow in our faith. The special rewards we indulge in become less important. It's less about the dessert and more about the real meal, the stuff that makes you happy and gives you peace.

In the NFL, players enjoy the camaraderie and the celebrations after a win, but mature Christians understand that overindulging in the wrong things ultimately won't provide the deep-down satisfaction we really need. The real gain is the peace in knowing we are truly following Christ by obeying God's commands, especially the most important one: to love God with all of our hearts and love our neighbor as we love ourselves (Matthew 22:37-39).

Yards to Go

The distance needed to obtain first down yardage. On every play, the offense is trying to reach the first down marker. The yards to go may vary to reach the goal.

After all of the hype and excitement following the signing of my first NFL contract, doubt took root and I stared ahead at the road on the way to New Orleans. A huge dream just came true, but would I have the talent, the strength, and ability to step out from the cusp of my dream and go the distance? Could I really make it in the NFL?

> *"Come," he said. Then Peter got down out of the boat, walked on the water and came toward Jesus. But when he saw the wind, he was afraid and, beginning to sink, cried out, "Lord, save me!" Immediately Jesus reached out his hand and caught him. "You of little faith," he said, "why did you doubt?" And when they climbed into the boat, the wind died down. Then those who were in the boat worshiped him, saying, "Truly you are the Son of God" (Matthew 14:29-33).*

When everything we've worked for is in sight, it's natural to catch our breath and question our ability to go the distance. Nothing about an NFL contract is solid and permanent, and I felt as though I were walking on water and could sink at any time.

But I'd played enough football to know that keeping a positive outlook when staring ahead at those yards to go is a must. You can never look down the field and say, "That's too much to gain." An entire team takes pride in gaining those yards by running and passing. Working together to move the ball those precious yards can be the most rewarding moments of the game, especially when they lead to a win.

In the Bible, Peter—knowing he couldn't walk on water through his own power—asked Jesus to tell him to come. He stepped out in faith but then noticed the wind, saw the troubled waters, and let fear grip him. With just a little way to go to get to Jesus, he took his eyes off of Him and nearly drowned.

If we ask Christ to lead us, He will beckon us to achieve things we could not otherwise imagine. A life of faith is about perseverance, taking risks, and moving forward knowing God is with us. But threats to our dreams, like the wind for Peter, can come in the form of self-doubt, a discouraging word from another, or a physical condition. Sin, like a penalty, can also set us back. When we look away from Jesus, we lose our ability to move forward.

Are you in troubled waters? Call on Jesus but don't doubt. When we, as Christians, commit ourselves, our plans, and our lives to God, we must trust that His power will sustain us as we press onward along the yards to go toward our goal.

If God's power can make miracles happen for a diabetic kid with a dream, it can happen for anyone. We should never take our eyes off our goals or off the One who beckons us to come.

(In the) Zone

Complete focus on a task, knowing how to
perfectly execute the plan to maximize the results
on any given play. In the zone, you don't allow
other factors to alter your performance.

After an intense year of living in four cities and playing for four different teams—being cut and then picked up, and being cut again and then picked up again—I finally finished the season in the playoffs with the San Diego Chargers. Staying in the zone all year had certainly paid off, but with the season over, I was ready for some Jake time. I thought I would maybe hit the beach and work on a tan.

Going out to grab some food with my friend Chris Marsh, I chatted about looking forward to being free from football stress, coaches' criticisms, and (happily single at the time) girlfriend drama.

Then, like Joe Frazier coming in with his famous left hook, the sight of a gorgeous blonde at the entrance of my favorite restaurant made my knees go weak. I turned to Chris and said, "I love her."

"Dibs."

"She's mine."

We both laughed as we sat down to eat. But I couldn't stop staring at her and talking about her. My gut sank down to my feet.

Chris looked over the top of his menu. "Go talk to her. I can't listen to you anymore."

Nervous, I made excuses.

As she walked toward our table, Chris stood, stopped her, and said, "Have you met Jake?"

She giggled, introduced herself, and—after Chris's persuasion—agreed to eat lunch with us.

Seek first his kingdom and his righteousness, and all these things will be given to you as well (Matthew 6:33).

Tyler Clutts, one of my good friends and teammate, once told me, "When you know, you know. If you have to ask yourself if she's the one, she's not."

When Emma Erickson smiled at me, Tyler's words returned and I just knew she was the one. After that day, I barely let her out of my sight. When I proposed nine months later, she said yes.

Being in the zone on the football field and in life is a good thing. It keeps us focused and on task moving toward our goals. We can map out our lives and stay in our zone, but being in God's zone is best. He knows exactly what each of us needs and when. He invites us to follow His master plan, which includes sending us the right person, the right job, and the answer to every prayer—all in His perfect time.

Extra Point

by Holly Michael

*After a touchdown, the offense has a chance to kick the
ball through the goal posts to earn an extra point, which
is also known as the point after touchdown or PAT.*

As I lay in the hospital bed, the doctor affirmed what I already knew. "You're miscarrying." He patted my hand and left the room.

Alone, I argued with God. He'd given me a strong, maternal nature. I wanted to be a mom above anything else. I already loved this baby. Why would He take my first child?

I wiped away tears as a nurse entered the room. Another pat on the hand. "Always have hope." She smiled and left, never examining me physically.

Given the cramps and immense loss of blood that passed all morning, hope seemed pointless. Nevertheless, I pondered on the nurse's encouraging word and then realized that hope meant giving a dire situation to God and trusting whatever outcome He chose. An extra point after the touchdown is always hoped for, but factors such as the wind or a quick, tall defensive player can mess up a well-intended kick. But, despite obstacles, the attempt is made.

Scared and sad, I made my attempt. I found a sliver of grace to lift my heart up to God and give the situation to Him completely. I dedicated the baby to Him. I prayed. "This child is Yours, Lord. Whatever the outcome, I trust in You. If I miscarry, I'll understand it was Your decision."

Immediately after my "amen" peace washed over me. The bleeding ceased. My baby was okay! Hearing the heartbeat for the first time brought tears of joy to my eyes and looks of surprise from the medical staff. (I never again saw that nurse who stopped in to comfort me.)

You have been my hope, Sovereign LORD, my confidence since my youth. From birth I have relied on you; you brought me forth from my mother's womb. I will ever praise you (Psalm 71:5-6).

A few months later, seated in a wheelchair in a hospital room, I looked into my newborn's eyes for the first time and gasped. He stared at me with eyes that carried what I can only describe as wisdom from heaven. He cooed. The moment stunned me. His coos came as a thank-you for my prayer. Then, just as suddenly, his gaze switched to that of an innocent newborn.

From that moment, I knew God had big plans for Jake's life, a purpose for which my prayers would play an important part.

Like the football soaring into the end zone for the extra point, hope—rising up to heaven—always brings the best result. It's never pointless.

About the Authors

Jake Byrne grew up in Rogers, Arkansas. A type 1 diabetic since age 14, he has since been proactive combating the disease and mentoring diabetic youth. He played football for the University of Wisconsin as a tight end and went on to compete in the NFL. Originally an undrafted free agent who signed with the New Orleans Saints in 2012, Jake has also been a Houston Texan, Kansas City Chief, and San Diego Charger.

Jake blogs at www.typewon.net

He can be reached through the following social media:
Facebook Page (Type Won): www.facebook.com/typewon1
Twitter: sugarfreejb82
Instagram: Jakebyrne81
Email: typewonquestions@gmail.com
Newsletter: http://eepurl.com/bgj7Pf

......

Holly Michael has enjoyed a writing career as a journalist, features writer, and a regular ghostwriter for *Guideposts* magazine before authoring several novels and nonfiction books.

Married to Anglican Bishop Leo Michael, Holly has three grown children: daughter Betsy and football-playing sons—Jake (NFL) and Nick (University of Louisiana-Lafayette).

Holly blogs at www.writingstraight.com

You can contact her at www.HollyMichael.com
Facebook @ http://www.facebook.com/AuthorHollyMichael or
Twitter: @HollyMichael
Newsletter: http://eepurl.com/5vTLP

To learn more about Harvest House books and
to read sample chapters, visit our website:

www.harvesthousepublishers.com

HARVEST HOUSE PUBLISHERS
EUGENE, OREGON